In her book YOU'LL NEVER Mastrodicasa brings importan to light along with personal anecdotes of how self-advocacy helps us transcend the most difficult of challenges. Through her personal life stories, readers will also connect how women supporting women can help create the life that they want. I know Maria from her philanthropy work, and as an advocate for people from diverse backgrounds, from impoverished circumstances to diplomatic leadership. Her book is a testimony for overcoming the obstacles in your life through the power of self-advocacy.

—Jim Sherlock, Founder and President of Reborn International.

"From growing up with undiagnosed dyslexia to rebuilding her life after enduring a heartbreaking divorce, and all the exciting ups and devastating downs in between, Maria Mastrodicasa has had multiple opportunities to learn the importance of self-advocacy and values for self, family and others. Her book provides valuable and usable lessons for women experiencing challenges at home and in the workplace that may initially feel insurmountable. I passionately support her for teaching women how to powerfully rise up against the challenges that come with all kinds of abuse, sexual harassment, and shame. This is the journey that Maria, along with so many other women, has experienced. She brings her stories to life in her book YOU'LL NEVER in a way that will motivate you to show the naysayers of life what you're actually made of."

—Jenna Ballard Cofounder of
Ascension Leadership Academy

"In her book YOU'LL NEVER; The Journey To What Is Possible, Maria Mastrodicasa brings important cultural, workplace and family topics to light along with personal anecdotes of how self-advocacy helps to transcend the most difficult of challenges. One of the things I love most, is that even when she was afraid, she knew to take a breath and face her fear head on. It's inspiring. Maria's passion for women's empowerment—for personal empowerment—is so palpable that it's sure to help any reader feel valued and supported in whatever life throws their way."

—Dallas Michael Cyr Creator of Igniting Your Purpose,
Mater Life Guide, Entrepreneur Mentor and Speaker

YOU'LL NEVER . . .

The Journey to What is Possible Through Self-Advocacy

Maria Mastrodicasa

Table of Contents

Dedication

This book is dedicated to my children and my cousin, Carmela.

I have always wanted children, a beautiful home with lots of children. I was blessed to have a beautiful, healthy boy and girl who I raised to be the kind of person I hoped the other would someday marry.

My son John is a kind, loving gentleman who loves everything sports, has a wonderful job, his own home. My daughter Amanda is a loving wife who cares deeply for her family and the home they've created. They make me so proud.

This book would not have come about if not for my dear cousin, Carmela. We grew up together, always having fun at each other's homes although I especially loved our sleepovers and dinners at her house.

Years later while working on Wall Street, I spoke to Carmela almost every day. I'd share with her all the craziness that went on at work and in my life, so she knew the good, the bad, and the ugly. It was when I was going through my most difficult times that Carmela would note, "Wow, this will make a great book someday," and then later, "That will be a good chapter for your book!"

I'm forever grateful to Carmela for always listening, giving great advice, being positive and helping me pull myself up to stand and self-advocate once again.

Here you have it, the book Carmela encouraged me to write.

Through the journey of writing this book, there have been others to thank: To Jenna and Brad Ballard for creating Ascension Leadership Academy (ALA), and to my ALA and SD5 family, I love each of you. To Alicia Dunams for her knowledge, support and guidance through the process of this book. To Dallas Michael Cyr for his intuitive, loving, authentic coaching and for igniting my purpose.

I thank you.

Foreword

Accomplishing what others told her was impossible, this Wall Street mogul, Maria Mastrodicasa, takes us through a journey of her life story, while making her journey to success evident throughout each chapter with exquisite vulnerability, transparency and grace.

From the moment I picked up the manuscript, I couldn't put it down. This book's timing is perfect! At a time when the world is searching for meaning, thirsty for role models, Maria shows us what it is like to live a life of values even in moments of uncertainty. Throughout the book she shares stories that help the reader learn what it's like to stand for their beliefs, while maintaining grace, faith, dignity and self-respect... and that of others.

Maria eloquently shares through her own stories, how self-advocacy has empowered her to push past all the "You'll Nevers..." to a life she envisioned for herself, and now for all women.

I found many similarities from my own life and that of so many women I have encountered throughout my travels, career and life journey. Every woman will be able to identify with so many situations in Maria's life, starting with her humble beginnings, learning about her dyslexia after going through a very trying childhood, working at a young age to support her family, embracing a life of faith, focusing on what truly matters, fighting for her own self-respect, being the only woman in a man's world, broken promises and a broken marriage, and finally, a sincere passion and commitment to help others overcome challenges and reach their own dreams through her role as a speaker and a coach.

The book is written in a format that lends itself to many forums for sharing and learning. Maria inserts key points throughout the book, making apparent the key lessons and tips, that will surely support women in recognizing limiting beliefs that lead to toxic behavior: their own, and that of others. She takes the reader through a "yellow brick road" that helps them create the steps to advocate for themselves with grace and dignity to achieve the results they want, in business and in life.

Maria's vulnerability makes each experience relatable, and an opportunity to learn and feel empowered. The common golden thread throughout the book is about speaking one's truth, serving as a North Star navigating life's unexpected turns while maintaining one's core values.

We all have a story; our upbringing, socioeconomic status, and geographic origins bring forth a series of situations that can cause us to get triggered as adults. As we see from Maria's experiences, when we are able to finally recognize our own value, we create the momentum to transform ourselves and the environment around us... this in turn leads to inevitable success.

After reading Maria's stories we leave inspired to advocate for ourselves and others around us. I highly recommend this book to every man and woman.

Dr. Betty™

CEO, Effectus Enterprises, dba Dr. Betty™. Past C-Executive in Finance and Commercial Banking; Global Influencer, Award-Winning Business Transformation Expert, Author, Speaker & Humanitarian; Ambassador for Peace and Human Rights (UNICEF, UN, OEA, CNDH, CDIH, USENSCO); FORBES Financial Council; International best-selling author of *#Values: The Secret to Top-Level Performance in Business & Life*; Award-winning corporate executive and transformational expert.

Introduction

I grew up in a nice area of Brooklyn. Most of the families in our neighborhood were Italian, Jewish and Irish. My family seemed to do very well. Our grandfather (my mother's father) was a contractor. He came over from Italy and built commercial and residential buildings and was a skilled tile worker as well. He brought over other family members who became successful in their own right. My sister and I always wore nice, new clothing and were taught to be respectful.

People tend to judge each other by their appearance and often don't see deeper issues when everything looks good on the surface. I was a well-dressed, well-mannered child. My surface was perfect, and I was truly happy.

Third grade was a turning point for me, and as I would learn later, that time was one of major change for my family as well. My father started a business in New Jersey and moved us there. He enrolled my sister and me into a private Catholic school, Our Lady Star of the Sea, and I thought it was going to be great. I was eager to attend my new school because my cousins went there.

One day, during class, Sister Frances, the teacher, asked me to stand up and read aloud from our book. This took me completely by surprise; it was something we had never been required to do back in my Brooklyn public school. If you've ever attended Catholic school, you know that no one ever questions a nun or tries to negotiate out of anything they ask you to do.

I stood up, smoothed my skirt, looked down at the page and began to read. The letters swam across the page and I struggled to speak the words they formed. I started and stopped and struggled. The other children in the class laughed at me, making my humiliation even worse.

Sister Frances finally ended my agony and allowed me to sit down, but told me I had to stay after school. When everyone else had left for the day, she called me up front and asked me if my parents knew that I couldn't read.

"Do you ever read to your parents? Do they help you with your homework?"

While I stood there, uncomfortable with all of her questions, she sat down at her desk, wrote a note, and sealed it in an envelope. She instructed me not to read the note and hand it directly to my parents when I arrived home that afternoon. I dutifully handed the note over to my mother, who read it and wrote a response, which I was never allowed to read either.

This experience really made me feel awful inside, because I just didn't understand what was happening. I thought, you know, maybe because I'm in a new school, things are different, or maybe Catholic school is stricter than public school?

This was just the first of many painful episodes I had with reading. Time and time again I would be instructed to read out loud, which of course I had to do. It then became a fear to read out loud. And is it any wonder? The nuns would literally hit me on the head with a book while I struggled. I was always in trouble.

Back then, and especially in Catholic school, children were to be seen and not heard. Even as a young child, I wondered why a school that was based on the word of God did not reflect the example of Jesus. The atmosphere was nothing at all like Him. Teachers and administrators displayed no compassion, no understanding and no love towards someone who needed help. The school, my family and I were all unaware I had a disability. This feeling stood with me at this age, and it is not okay with me that authority figures treat any child poorly, especially when they have the power to help them.

The nuns did not offer to help me or tutor me. On each report card, my effort would be marked "satisfactory." Yet, at the end of the year, the nuns said they were leaving me back, and I'd have to repeat third grade. Without help, how would my reading level go up? I felt horrible. My father placed me in a public school the next year where I repeated the third grade. The teachers were much nicer there, and my stay only lasted a few months. During that year, my mother, my sister and I moved back to Brooklyn, and I was enrolled in yet another public school. Three schools for third grade. This certainly didn't help with my reading issues.

It was only after I became an adult and had landed a job on Wall Street that a tutor told me I had dyslexia. Dyslexia is a learning difference that makes it difficult for people to read and write. When I was a child, dyslexia was unheard of. If a child struggled with reading, or any other type of learning difference, they were considered "dumb" and in many cases, "unteachable."

The house my grandfather built

**The photo is of my grandfather with my
Mother and Father**

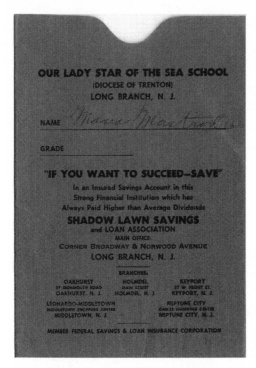

Our Lady Star of The Sea School

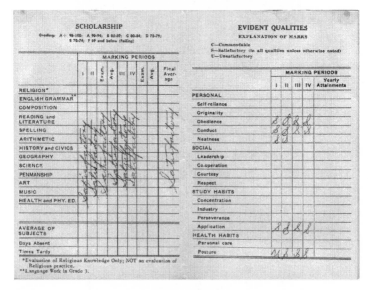

Report Card

"You'll Never"

This wasn't just a struggle at school. It became a struggle at home. When I was 10 years old, my father remarried a woman with two daughters. One afternoon I overheard my father's wife nagging at my father, and, being a child, I shamelessly listened in and discovered they were discussing me!

I overheard her say, "Maria will never be anything. My children are going to be teachers and successful, and Maria is never going to amount to anything. She can't even read!"

I would hear the words, "**You'll Never**," many times over.

You'll never amount to anything. **You'll never** learn how to read. **You'll never** have thin thighs. **You'll never** be able to get a job in New York. **You'll never** be a broker. **You'll never** make it on Wall Street. **You'll never** have a custom-built home. **You'll never** leave me. **You'll never** make it on your own. **You'll never** keep the kids. **You'll never** win this lawsuit.

The words were painful enough, but the greatest pain was my father's non-reaction that day. He didn't say one word in my defense. Not a word uttered from his lips. He never said, "Don't say that about my daughter. Don't be silly, Maria's smart. Maybe she just has difficulty reading."

Clearly, he shared her opinion of my abilities . . . and my future.

Despite the revelation of how my father and his wife saw me, I just always thought anything was possible. I had dreams, and my focus was on those end points, the type of life I wanted, the type of job I wanted, the type of house I wanted. It never occurred to me to imagine any of the pitfalls or challenges between me and my dreams. My determination was going to take me there.

Looking back, I should really thank my father's wife for what she said that day. Did you ever see the movie *Matilda*? Based on the book by Roald Dahl, the protagonist is Matilda, a first grader who does not come from a very supportive family either. And while my parents weren't mean, Matilda's sure were. Not only did they think she was useless and stupid, they treated her like she was standing in the way of their happiness. One day, while Matilda's father was yelling at her and threatening to hit her, Matilda realized her power. She realized she was magic and could be and do anything she wanted. From that day forward, Matilda knew she had the ability to handle whatever challenges life threw at her.

Matilda's magic power was the ability to move objects with her mind. Little Maria Mastrodicasa's magic was belief in herself, something far more powerful. That day, overhearing that awful conversation, was the beginning of my journey—my journey of self-advocacy.

I wrote this book in the hope it will help even one person. I really want each person who reads this book to know that they are beautiful and worthy from the inside out. And I want them to truly feel that. There were many times when I did not feel that way, and it has been a long journey for me.

As you read about my life, you may recognize yourself in some of these stories. You may have gone through something similar. If you have gotten through to the other side, then we stand there together, stronger, wiser as inspiring examples to others. If today, you are in the midst of living through challenging circumstances, perhaps my story will give you hope—seeing that even a little girl with big dreams, can triumph over adversity to create a fulfilling life. And if you are just starting out in life? May your life be blessed with a strong circle of friends and family who support you on your journey. And maybe my stories will serve as a warning so that you may avoid some of the pitfalls I struggled through. May you recognize them before you ever fall victim, and may my words be those that you share with others to help them along the way.

I write this book ...

Because right now, there is someone out there with a wound the exact shape of your words.

"Why Bother," a poem by Sean Thomas Dougherty (from Brooklyn), from his book, *The Second O of Sorrow.*

Part One

Come with me as I tell you about my life growing up in Brooklyn. You will follow me to school and watch as I build my career from the ground up. You'll join me as I break into the men's club that is Wall Street; and perhaps you'll cry with me as I recount the collapse of my marriage and my experiences with litigation.

Maybe you will recognize yourself in some of my stories, struggles and triumphs. None of us travel this world alone, and I am writing this book to let you know you are not alone either.

Chapter 1. Secrets

"The costs of keeping secrets include our growing isolation due to fear of detection and the ways we shut down inside to avoid feeling the effects of our behavior. We can never afford to be truly seen and known—even by ourselves."

—Sharon Salzberg, *Real Love: The Art of Mindful Connection*

In the summer of 1970, we were all busy getting on with life. I had to adapt to three schools, two new neighborhoods, two moves, new friends, new rules, new expectations. We were all living in a big secret, which only years later did I recognize as a family pattern.

When I was little, my parents loaded me in the car and told me we were going to get ice cream. The real destination was to the hospital where I was to have my tonsils removed. No warning. No nothing. Just, "We're going for a ride." My parents had known for weeks that I was going and had kept it a secret from me.

When our family moved to New Jersey, it was handled in the same way; my sister and I were told, "Let's go for a ride to see your cousins." And the next thing we know, we are living in a different house. We were never given the opportunity to prepare or even say goodbye to our friends.

Once we moved to New Jersey, my father got very busy with work. At least that is what I was told. My sister and I would wake up in the morning to get ready for school, and our mother would tell us that Dad had already left for work. The afternoon I brought the letter home from the nun, only my mother read it. She said that Dad wouldn't be getting home until after we had gone to bed.

I didn't see my father for days, but he did spend most weekends with us. My world kept rolling along. I loved playing with my cousins, and other than my increasing fear of reading aloud, I enjoyed school. When the weather was nice, I would play outside after school. And on the weekends, we would visit my cousins and my mom would spend time with our aunt Angie. Sometimes, my cousins and I would go to the church to watch funny movies, like the Nutty Professor with Jerry Lewis.

But, I did not like the home my parents bought in New Jersey. It was not like our home in Brooklyn. My parents rented two parts of a three-family home, and we lived upstairs. It was small, dark, and my sister and I had bunk beds with cork board on the wall that smelled awful. I can still smell it, and it was unpleasant. The family only came to visit once in a while in the summer since they all had summer homes on Long Island, which I loved!

It was years later before I understood what was really happening that year. From the time we arrived in New Jersey, my father started seeing another woman, and very quickly moved in with her. My mother never said a word about this to my sister and me. Another secret. She ran the house alone and covered for his absence. Divorce was not talked about in those days. The pressure must have been unbearable on my mother, to suffer her heartbreak in silence and keep up appearances for her children and the outside world.

The stress began to take its toll on my mother. My sister and I were too young to realize we were watching our sweet, hard-working mother crumble into a nervous breakdown. From what little she confided in her sisters, they were able to recognize that the three of us needed help.

One Tuesday, my mother's sisters came over to the house. This was very unusual, because they lived far away, and they had their own families to take care of. My aunts packed the car and loaded our dog Rusty in the back seat. They had stuffed all they could into the trunk of my aunt's Cadillac, and they drove my mother, sister and me back across the Verrazano Bridge to Brooklyn. I remember the drive was very quiet; my aunts were not saying very much, only that we were going to Grandma's.

I was happy to be going to my grandmother's and was excited to see so many of my friends who lived on the same block. More than 30 years later, I can still recall how her house smelled. Grandmother was a wonderful cook, and the minute you walked in the front door of her immaculate house you could smell the tempting scents of fresh food coming from the kitchen. She made wonderful soups, veal and chicken cutlets, lamb chops, fresh vegetables, and salad every evening, pasta and more. When I was sick, she would bring me food on a tray to my room and have me sit up so that she could put the tray down and sit with me while I ate.

I loved being back in Brooklyn and settled into my third school with surprising ease. The teachers didn't terrorize me, and I managed to stay under the radar. The school just pushed me along to the next grade, and the next, without ever addressing my reading problem. When not standing in front of the class, I wasn't afraid to read and actually enjoyed the stories, but I would stick to books that I could read without too much challenge. My favorite was Dr. Seuss's Green Eggs and Ham, and I read it over and over.

Already, I was compensating for my reading weakness by sticking to limited choices I could negotiate. I wasn't overcoming; I was adapting.

And while life was progressing for me as it was for the other grade school children, it was becoming more unbearable for my mother. Mom had been a very social woman. She used to have lots of friends. She played cards and Mahjong and loved to dance. Once we moved into Grandma's, my mother became very quiet. She stopped seeing her friends and engaging in the activities that she once loved. Instead she slept. Each day marked a deeper retreat into her personal darkness. Her mood, her depression, descended over the house like a heavy velvet curtain at the end of a play.

My mother, sister Angela and me

My parents, sister Angela and me

My dad leaning on his car

My mother

This is one of my favorite photos. My dad would always surprise my sister and me with toys, dolls and other gifts. Girraffs are one of my favorite animals

My grandmother's house, which always represented happiness to me, was now filled with a tangible sadness—a foreboding that crept across the floorboards and up our legs until we were all on edge. Along with the sadness was fear. My grandmother watched helplessly as her daughter fell deeper and deeper into her despair over her broken marriage. Grandma was afraid my mother would take her own life. This time marked the beginning of a series of breakdowns my mother would suffer for many years.

I did not see my dad much during that time. My mother's family told him to stay away so that my mom would have time to adapt and hopefully heal from his betrayal.

We stayed with my grandmother for less than a year. Eventually, my mother was somehow able to pull herself up out of the abyss and began adjusting to living without my father. Our family had been a blessed support system for Mom, and she was strong enough, once again, to stand on her own two feet. Still, she wasn't the mom I used to know; some days were up, and some were down, and she remained withdrawn. Eventually she decided that we needed a place of our own.

I didn't want to leave my grandmother's. Why would I? It was nice there and my friends were there, but my mother said it was time to go. She packed up my sister and me, and moved us to an apartment in East Flatbush, near avenue D in Brooklyn, and closer to my aunts. Then we moved to Bay Ridge, and we moved again, and again. I can't count the number of apartments. We moved too much.

Lessons Learned. Watching my mother's struggle, her weakness, and her breakdowns made me reflect when I was faced with my own marital challenges. I made a conscious decision that I was not going to allow myself to crumble in the same way she had. I would be strong for myself and my children.

Chapter 2. School Was Not for Me

"The only thing that interferes with my learning is my education."

—Albert Einstein

I had to take a bus from where I lived out to Meyer Levin Junior High School in the East Flatbush section of Brooklyn, New York. The whole experience was scary and very dangerous. It was there I was told "**You'll never**," for the first time. "Maria, if you don't read this…" "Maria, if you do not do this, or that, **you'll never** graduate!"

I was put in special classes. In my first few weeks and months I tried to do all I was told. I wanted to learn; I sat in the front of the class so I could hear the teacher and pay attention because I was truly interested. Mr. Rappaport was the English teacher. He would not yell at me but challenge me. He would teach me and have me take my time pronouncing words. I liked how that felt. He was also the Dean, which was really helpful, because he had a great deal of control of how I functioned at school.

One time I did not complete an assignment, and he wanted to punish me. He decided to keep me out of a school performance that I had been practicing with the fellow students. I was to sing Carol King's "You've Got a Friend." He forbade me to perform, but my fellow students convinced me to go on anyway. And, go on I did. I sang as he stood in the back of the assembly room. Yes, I get it. I should not have gone on. As soon as I got off stage, he called me to his office. He called my mother and told her he wanted to suspend me, but he wasn't going to "since that is what Maria wants." I do believe, however, that I was more respected by my classmates after that act of defiance.

After a while, going to school was more about survival. The teachers were mostly babysitting the students, unable to teach, basically pushing everyone through the system as long as they passed the statewide reading test. I felt great fear when that test came around each year. Not because I feared failing. I feared that if I did not pass the 9th grade, I'd be stuck there in that very dangerous school forever. Although I am a bit embarrassed, the truth is that I was reading at the 4th grade level when I was in the 9th grade.

I thought, how on earth can I get my reading level from 4th grade to a 9th grade for this statewide, timed reading test? Even though the nun in 3rd grade told me I could not read, I knew I could. It just took me a lot longer than others. I felt bad about that. I did not know why I struggled, and she made me feel bad about myself—like something was wrong with me.

I asked for help from one of the teachers and he agreed to work with me for some time before the test. I was still very nervous. He told me if I run out of time, guess, and don't leave one question blank. I did all he suggested and ... Yes! I passed the statewide reading test! I was so surprised and shocked. I did it! I did it! And now I can, and I will, graduate ... or so I thought.

The principal sent for me. I am thinking, "What now?" I went to his office and sat down. He asks me all types of questions. "How did you pass this test?" "How is it possible that you took your reading level from 4th to 9th grade?"

I told the truth and said I did the best I could then ran out of time, "so I guessed the rest of the answers." He said, "You guessed and were able to do that well?"

At this point I was confused and frustrated, and it showed in my response with a bit of an attitude. Well the principal was not happy with me and he said, "You'll have to take the test again!"

I took a breath. Yes, back then, I knew to take a breath. I was nervous and fearful of speaking up, but I calmly asked, "Are you telling me I have to take this test, this statewide test, over? If so, then I will request that every student be required to retake this test."

I continued, and before he could reply, told him, "Let's face it, we know I guessed through most of the test and I was lucky. Next time, I may not be as lucky and I want to know if you can single me out on such a test."

He looked upset by the way I challenged him. For me this was about survival. There was no one to advocate for me that day in the

Junior High Report Card

principal's office. I had to speak up for myself. Thankfully, I was not forced to retake the test and graduated!

In addition to the reading challenges, I had to deal with a school that was so dangerous, the children who took the bus from our neighborhood would cut school to stay safe. I was attacked on numerous occasions and one of the teachers was even stabbed that year.

Junior high school was also when harassment started for me. I was attacked multiple times, in the bathroom, and the gym locker room, where I was pushed, threatened to get beat up after school. Then worse while I was walking down the hall; I was grabbed from behind and molested. I was terrified, and I don't know where the nerve came from, but I heard myself snarling, "You don't know who you are dealing with!"

I went straight to Dean Rappaport, and thankfully, the school had surveillance cameras. I found the boy and pointed him out. The dean brought him back to his office, and we got the boy to admit it.

13

The dean strongly warned the boy to never bother me again and to tell his friends the same. I was in fear of what he and other boys may do. The dean then suggested that I not go to school on the days he was not there, he would let me know the day before or call our home to let my mother know. I think he feared for me that the boy and his friends may do something more than molest me. He also gave me a key to the teachers' lounge so I could use that bathroom instead of the student bathrooms.

When I told my mother and begged her to allow me to go to a different school, it was like talking to a brick wall. Her only response was an exasperated, "Oh, Maria." I don't know if she didn't take me seriously or simply did not want to deal with the situation. I was afraid to go to school after the incident with the boy.

1979, my first year of high school, was a year of upheaval just about everywhere. Jimmy Carter was president. A reactor fire at the Three Mile Island nuclear power plant released radiation into the Pennsylvania countryside. And in November, more than 3,000 Iranian radicals and students stormed the U.S. Embassy in Iran and held 60 people hostage for 444 days.

My friends and I were listening to the newest music, which I still love today. Michael Jackson released "Don't Stop 'til You Get Enough." We sang along with Donna Summer's "Hot Stuff." Everybody was dancing to "Le Freak," and Gloria Gaynor released "I Will Survive," which has become an inspirational anthem for many women.

By this time, I was zoned to attend Erasmus Hall High School on Flatbush Avenue in Brooklyn. We always heard this was the most dangerous school in Brooklyn. People said it was ten times worse than Meyer Levin where I had just graduated.

Now it was my turn for secrets. Given my mother's lack of response to the junior high school violence, I had no faith she would intercede on my behalf in high school either. I only pretended to go to school.

I would get up each morning and get ready for school, and once my mom and sister left for work, I headed back to bed. Sometimes, I would do something else, like draw or do crafts. By the second quarter though, I begged my mom to please sign me out of school, not because I didn't want to learn. I love to learn. It was the danger. I did not see the point in putting myself in such situations if I was not going to learn.

It was then that my mother, without me knowing, called my dad and they made a plan that I would live with him, his wife and her family to complete school.

Mom sent me to live with my dad, maybe to relieve herself of any responsibility of having to deal with the situation

It was the second quarter of 10th grade. Again, I am the new girl. I signed up for my classes and was looking forward to them, especially music class, which I always enjoyed.

One day after music class, three girls followed me out of the school and were making fun of me, calling me names, touching their hair saying, "Oh, I'm so cool (meaning me); I'm from Brooklyn," and so on. I felt a little afraid, and then I turned around and said, "Listen, I came here to learn. I have dealt with worse than you in Brooklyn, so if you want to fight, (which I was apprehensive to say) let's get it over with." They stopped walking toward me and said, "No, no, we want to be friends." That completely diffused the situation and, later on, we did become friends.

I attend my first English class, sat down, and there was a vinyl record player. The teacher said we were going to listen to Shakespeare. When the record finished, the teacher said we are going to go around the room and take turns reading. I think to myself, "Are you kidding? Shakespeare out loud?" The teacher called on me. I thought to myself, "I'm the new girl. Do I read and get laughed at by my peers once again?"

She called on me again, and I said, "I am sorry, I cannot read today and can talk with you after class." She said, "Maria, you read or go to the principal's office." Now, I don't recommend this, but I gathered my things and started walking toward the door. The teacher asked sternly, "Where do you think you're going?" I was not trying to be disrespectful, but answered honestly, "to the principal's office." She told me to sit back down. She really did not want me to bother the principal over this. Despite this incident, most teachers treated me well.

I was very glad I did not read that day. Many of the students came up to me and introduced themselves after that class. I do not think that would have happened had I read aloud. Although I did not do very well academically, I was polite and that is why I think the teachers treated me nicely.

Every day, I would leave the frustration of my new school to go home to a completely alien environment.

My father's wife was not interested in housekeeping or cooking; consequently, their house was not very clean. It was hard to adjust to since my parents' home in Brooklyn was extremely clean and organized. Heck, our sheets were sent out to be cleaned and pressed weekly. When my dad's wife did try to prepare a meal, her efforts consisted solely of heating up some frozen food, and food that I was not familiar with, so Dad did most of the cooking. She would not allow me to eat the things I enjoyed, even if I offered to pay for them. Actually, it would infuriate her, and she would tell me, "Maria, maybe you have too much money for your age to think you can buy different food." At that time, I did not eat meat on Fridays, being a Catholic, and asked to buy tuna fish. You'd think I was asking for caviar the way she spoke to me.

The house I grew up in with my parents was a pretty calm and respectful environment. If my parents got upset with my sister or me, they'd give us a look, or use a certain tone of voice. My parents never raised a hand to us. When my parents had disagreements between themselves, they would have what they called "discussions." My sister and I would try to listen through the door to these discussions, but our parents spoke so softly we could barely hear anything they were saying.

Life with my father's new family was like nothing I had ever witnessed, absolutely beyond my imagination. I had never even seen anything like it, even on television.

This woman was awful to her daughters. She would scream at them, hit them, and rip the hair out of their heads while dragging them down the steps. It was crazy to me. I liked her daughters and they never did anything to deserve this type of behavior. No child does.

Another time his wife was chasing her oldest daughter down the stairs. I thought, "Oh no, not again." A little while later, I heard her beating on her daughter's bedroom door, screaming, "Let me in!" A few minutes after that, there was a horrendous banging and ripping sound.

I peeked out my door to see what was happening, and she was using an axe! Yes, an axe to break in.

Eventually, my father's wife started to take things out on me, too. It began with her complaining to my father that I would never amount to anything since I couldn't read. She next tried to turn Dad against me by making up stories then telling him he needed to punish me by not allowing me out of the house. This way, she would have me there to babysit her children before and after school.

I heard one of these stories when my dad came to me and said that he heard I was making out with a boy in the hallway at school. I had no reason or thought to do that. I was there to learn and get the heck back to Brooklyn with my family and friends. So, I advocated for myself with a question, "Where did you hear this?" I was not afraid of his answer, as I knew the story was not true.

He said his wife was at the grocery store and ran into her friend who was a teacher at the school. I said, "Really? That's interesting. It's not true."

His response was, "Why would she tell me that?" I knew what her motivation was, but I chose not to share that with him, nor did I share what I decided to do next. I did not sleep that night and the next morning, before class, I walked into this teacher's room. We had never met, and not being a student in her class, she asked if she could help me. I introduced myself. "Hi, I am Maria Mastrodicasa." I told her who my father's wife was, and that she told him that she ran into you the other day at the grocery store.

She said, "Maria I have not seen her in three months." Yes, very interesting indeed. I nodded politely and, very happily thanked her. The rest of the day I spent not paying attention in class and wondering why an adult would make up such a thing about any child. What would she gain?

Her campaign to tear me down in my father's eyes continued. This was the '70s and movies like *Saturday Night* Fever and *Grease* were influencing the clothing styles. My father's wife called him into the kitchen. "Tom, could you come in here? Maria's home from school and look what she's wearing. She looks like a slut."

Well I don't think I ever heard that word or at least not said to me. I'm thinking, "What now? I'm into fashion."

Before he could say anything, which I was sure he would not, I said, "This is the style!" I thought I looked cool wearing jeans with a bodysuit and a jacket on top. His wife turns red in the face, and I could feel her anger rising. My dog Rusty, always protective, came right by my side, because he too could feel the tension in the kitchen rising. She pointed her finger at me, screaming in my face, "That's your style?"Rusty started barking and barking. My dad could not stop him, so put him outside.

I wasn't her only target. My dad's wife would get into fights with him like I'd never seen. The incident that stands out the most is the time she came running up from her office downstairs and stormed into the bedroom she and my dad shared. It sounded like they were having a conversation at first; then she started yelling. My father's wife began screaming, over and over, "Go ahead, hit me. Hit me!" I was thinking, "Oh my goodness, she is crazy, and I have to get out of here ASAP!"

Sadly, my father did hit her in the stomach. She could not catch her breath. This drama had escalated to violence and become very scary to me. Her mother came up and told all of us kids to go outside, while she made attempts to calm her down.

After this episode, I called my mother and sister and told them about the things that were going on in that house. They thought I was exaggerating. I wish I was. When I told Mom that I wanted to come home, she responded, "Oh, Maria," as if she didn't believe me.

I no longer felt it was in my best interest to stay living with my father and his wife. It was not a healthy environment. I tried to tell my mom and my sister. I mean, who would make this stuff up? I was not looking for attention. I only wanted two things: to learn, and to be back in a place I could be myself and be safe. My mom was very easy going for the most part. All she wanted was to know who I was with, for me to be home on time, or call when I was going to be late.

It was time to self-advocate again. I begged my mom and basically told her I that I was not safe in that house and she must come get me. My mom did not drive so, she had her friend, Marie, drive her to come pick me up. She knew Marie could handle my dad's wife and we'd leave with no problem. That is how I moved back in with my mother.

Once back in Brooklyn, Mom gave me two choices. Go back to school or get a job. I did not even hesitate. School was not for me. It was miserable, violent, and I certainly wasn't learning anything.

I've always had a strong belief in myself and never doubted for a minute I would succeed in creating the life I wanted. This was a time when women were gaining more visibility. The year before, President Jimmy Carter had established the National Advisory Committee for Women. Margaret Thatcher became Great Britain's first female prime minister. And Tracy Austin was all over the news for becoming the youngest national women's U.S. Open tennis champion at age 16.

Movies and television were full of aspirational role models. Sally Field was a union organizer in *Norma Rae*. There were predominantly female casts in a number of television programs, including *The Facts of Life* and *Laverne & Shirley*. *Charlie's Angels* was a huge influence on all young girls at the time. Who didn't want to be a tough, fashionable crime-fighter with Farrah Fawcett hair? *The Jeffersons*, *The Love Boat*, and *Dallas* all reflected aspirational lifestyles.

I left school, never completing 10th grade and was ready to take on the world. I was going to be a businesswoman.

I had made friends easily in high school, but my world changed the minute I got hired at the first brokerage firm where I worked. I talked with the kids from New Jersey from time to time on the phone after I left, but those relationships, eventually and naturally, faded away. I still saw my Brooklyn friends, but my new life was so rewarding, and I did not miss the things my former classmates were engaged in. While they were attending prom, I was attending board meetings.

Lessons Learned. I cannot count on people in positions of power to help me when decency dictates they should. I cannot expect support or encouragement from the people closest to me. I get to be my own advocate.

Chapter 3. The Sheep of Wall Street

"The most valuable commodity I know of is information."
—Gordon Gekko, *Wall Street*

If Leonardo DiCaprio was the Wolf of Wall Street, I was the Sheep.

I have been working since I was 14 and have never been shy to try something new. I would take the bus to work in Brooklyn, and in a matter of a few years I had worked in sales at a men's and children's shoe store, for extended family at a bridal salon, and at an art corporation shipping storyboards, Marvel comics and other artwork all over the world.

These jobs honed my sales skills, my people skills, and my secretarial skills. At each place I worked, I developed more confidence in myself and realized new goals. These were all respectable, steady jobs, and many people would have been satisfied to settle in with the steady employment they provided, especially as a teenager with no high school diploma. As my confidence grew, my dreams grew bigger.

Then I got a job at a tool corporation doing clerical work and learned how to use their new computer system. It was nice working there because it was local, which was convenient. But it didn't pay very well and, truthfully, I was bored. I told my sister, who also worked there, "I think I am going to take this token I use for the bus and instead take a train into NYC." This was the '80s and the token was like a Metro card today. I thought with that token, instead of getting on the bus to go to the other side of Brooklyn to make a little bit of money, I would go to Manhattan and make a lot more.

In a way, with each new stepping stone of accomplishment, I grew a bit deafer to the voices of discouragement. Oh, they were still there, and the comments were painful for me to hear, but my determination and my faith in myself helped me ignore the "**you'll nevers**."

My sister did not seem to understand my ambition. I said, "I can make more money in Manhattan." I don't remember if she actually used the words "**you'll never**," but it sure felt as though she did. I told my mom, who worked in Manhattan, about my plans, and she just said, "Oh Maria, where will you go?" Back then there was no Google to search for companies or job opportunities.

My mother and sister had a lot to say about my plan, and none of it was positive. "Oh Maria, what can you do without a diploma?" "**You'll never** get a job in the city." "Who is going to hire you?" I was hoping for a little encouragement or for them to believe in me, so I had to advocate for myself.

Searching through the Yellow Pages (the business phone book), I found Dover Employment Agency, and decided, "I am going there." They were on Broadway in NYC. I still remember what I wore the day I went: a white cotton shirt, a skirt with a thin navy and black plaid pattern from JCPenney, black shoes, and a bag to match.

I had two interviews. One was with the manager, and then I was to meet the owner, Pete. Yes, they hired me. I still have a poetry book Pete gave me, congratulating me on the great job I was doing after

Dover Employment Agency

my first month. I really enjoyed it there, making friends and being in Manhattan. I learned a lot. Helping people get placed in a job they wanted was fulfilling.

Things started to slow down, and a colleague asked me if I would go on some interviews for her. They were mostly jobs for which I was not qualified. I agreed to go on the interviews anyway, looking at it as a great learning experience, and it really was. I never again was nervous on an interview.

One day I saw a job listing for a trainee position at a brokerage firm. No experience needed. Wow, how perfect! I could work on the trading floor! How cool is that, I thought, and asked my colleague to please set up an interview. "Are you sure, Maria?" she asked.

"Yes, I am sure."

I was very excited for the interview and went home to tell my sister and my mother. They asked, "Why not stay at the employment agency?" I started telling them that at the employment agency I was paid commission only. If I did not place someone, I did not get paid. "This new job is a trainee position at a brokerage firm on Wall Street!"

My mom said in that disapproving tone, "Mariiiiaaaaa, you don't even have a diploma, **you'll never** be able to get a real job without a diploma!" I wanted to put my head down and walk away I felt so bad. Instead I cooked dinner and didn't mention it again.

The next day I went to work at the employment agency, and later that afternoon I went to the brokerage firm. I interviewed with Vinny, the president of the company. He glanced at my resume and said, "Maria Mastrodicasa, you're hired! You're Italian and we are Italian. You're hired!"

I was surprised that he did not read my resume. So, I asked him, "Don't you want to read my resume?"

He said, "All you need to do at this point is be here every day, on time and be able to put up with locker room talk." He told me what the salary and bonus would be in the first year. Vinny offered me $19,000 plus full medical and dental benefits, and a bonus. Not to mention free breakfast and lunch. It seemed to be a lot for someone (as my mom stated) who did not have a high school diploma. This was when the average salary was $17,500 and women were earning an average of 62% of their male counterparts, around $550 a week.

I had hit it out of the park the first time at bat. Not really knowing what I was in for I said, "Yes!"

I was officially hired for my first brokerage job with Fundamental Brokers Incorporated. We used to answer the phone "FBI" until the actual FBI came and taped our phone calls during an investigation.

FBI brokered government-backed securities, T-bills, Notes, and Bonds. They were the number one government bond broker with 300 employees, expanding to nearly 1,000 in just a few years. Brokerage houses put buyers and sellers together anonymously and receive a commission.

The New York Times described brokerage houses in the June 9, 1983 article entitled *Big 5 U.S. Securities Dealers*: (https://www.nytimes. com/1983/06/09/business/big-5-us-securities- dealers.html):

> Wall Street is full of middlemen whose business is to bring buyers and sellers together and extract a profit along the way. In the Treasury market, the world's largest securities market, with more than five times the dollar volume of the New York Stock Exchange, middlemen have carved a special niche. Because there is no central trading floor for Treasury issues, a handful of little-known broker firms have evolved to execute trades between securities firms.

At FBI, my position was assistant broker. I did well for someone without a diploma, as I was reminded by my mom, and all the boys and men made way more than any women did at that time.

I worked on the trading floor listening to the bids and offers of the notes, bonds, etc. - all government securities. It was my job to type in what I heard within seconds. I also wrote on an overhead projector.

When I started, I was amazed at all the action, energy and intelligence flying around the room. Men from Yale, Harvard and Wharton were everywhere. Ivy Leaguers. Inside I was glowing, remembering all the "**you'll nevers**," and there I was, working on the trading floor of the government's market. I thought, "Now I am here!"

Wall Street in the '80s was just like the movies *The Wolf of Wall Street* and *Wall Street*. It was a hedonistic cocktail of drugs, corruption, sex and money. Everybody was making money—from the Jordan Belforts at the top, to me, an assistant broker on a much lower rung.

Special instructions for _____
Your name (PLEASE PRINT)

You have already indicated the following deferral instructions based
upon your response to a memorandum early this fiscal year:

Current Bonus _____ 100 %

Defer to January 1983 _____0_____ %

Total _____ 100 %

Option A:

Please withhold taxes as follows:

Federal _____%, instead of 20%

New York State _____%, instead of 5%

New York City _____%, instead of 1.8% resident, or .45% non-resident

————————————————OR————————————————

Option B:

Please withhold the following additional lump sums:

Federal $_____

New York State $_____

New York City $_____

Other Special Instructions:

_____

_____

_____

_____

_____

Signed:_____

Work Documentation

I worked with the wolves, and yes there were drugs everywhere.
I chose not to partake and that was frowned upon. The drug lifestyle
never interested or tempted me; I could see how it made people behave
and lose control, and I was very serious about my career. The real FBI
came and tapped our phones to find out more about the drugs being

25

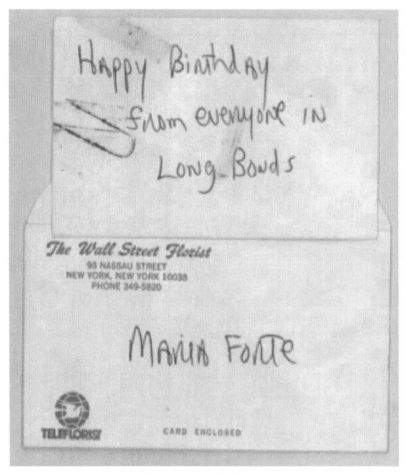

Birthday card from floral arrangement

given to ladies, co-workers and clients. Was it for fun, or to bribe clients to do business with them, or both?

Despite the craziness and male-dominated landscape, from the moment I walked in the door of the trading room floor, I never felt like I didn't belong. However, it was after two weeks or so on the job that I realized I was going to need help with my reading. I wanted to make sure I'd keep this exciting job.

EMPLOYMENT AGREEMENT

AGREEMENT made this September 24, 1987 between GARBAN Ltd., a New York corporation, (the "Company"), with principal offices at 120 Broadway, New York, New York 10271 and MARIA FORTE (the "Employee").

In consideration of the mutual convenants and agreements herein contained and for other good and valuable consideration, the receipt and sufficiency whereof is hereby acknowledged, the parties hereby agree as follows:

1. Employment, Acceptance and Term

1.1 Subject to the terms and conditions of this Agreement, the Company hereby agrees to employ the Employee and the Employee hereby agrees to serve the Company.

1.2 The term of this Agreement shall commence on October 1, 1987 and end on September 30, 1988.

2. Duties and Authority

During the term of this Agreement, the Employee shall devote his full time and energies to the business and affairs of the

Garban Employment Agreement

15. Captions

All captions and headings herein contained are inserted for convenience of reference only and shall not affect the meaning or interpretation of this Agreement.

IN WITNESS WHEREOF, the parties have executed this Agreement as of the day and year first above written.

GARBAN LTD.

By: _____
Stephen R. Tilton

By: _____
Maria Forte

Garban Employment Agreement

I called a family doctor, Dr. Ralph Lopez, who was head of cardiology (and also a doctor in psychology) at New York Hospital, and asked, "Do you know anyone who could help tutor me?" He gave me the name of a good friend of his.

A couple of times a week I would travel from Brooklyn on the train to the upper east side and sit in this woman's kitchen and she would teach me the skills I needed to improve my reading. Then I would jump back on the train downtown to my office. She's the one who said, "Maria I know what your difficulty is. You're dyslexic."

"What is that?" I had no idea what it was, and she explained it to me in detail. According to the International Dyslexia Association, "Dyslexia is a specific learning disability that is neurobiological in origin. It is characterized by difficulties with accurate and/or fluent word recognition and by poor spelling and decoding abilities. These difficulties typically result from a deficit in the phonological component of language that is often unexpected in relation to other cognitive abilities and the provision of effective classroom instruction. Secondary consequences may include problems in reading comprehension and reduced reading experience that can impede growth of vocabulary and background knowledge."

I said to the tutor, "So you mean I am not an idiot, and I can learn to read better?" She assured me that I was not, and that I could. I did all that she suggested with fervor.

People at my office offered to help and gave me books so I may better understand the government market. I decided to take non-credit classes in business and political economics at NYU so I could learn and better understand. I felt like a kid again!

I subscribed to the *Wall Street Journal* and the New York *Times*. Every day I would go into work an hour early with my big King James Version of the Bible and read things to help me improve my skills. Colleagues saw me with that big Bible, and they'd make fun of me. But I would read the Bible because it's difficult to read the King James Version and I wanted to challenge myself.

I also fasted on Mondays, drinking only water, juice and some coffee. I still do intermittent fasting to give my digestive track a break. It also gives me clarity and helps with focus, cleanses the organs and helps with longevity.

I was asked about the fasting often, but the reading of the Bible was what people made the most fun of. I solved that by getting a condensed version.

I also got clear about my goals. I decided that I would do whatever it took and worked really hard learning how to read, to understand, to comprehend. My new skills got me very, very excited, and I felt after watching everyone on the trading floor that I too could do it. How hard could it be?

I was so excited that I shared my dreams with some of the men who were brokers on the floor, and they looked at me and laughed. They said, "Maria, it's a man's world. You are lucky you are invited in. You don't get ahead unless you give it." I just didn't know what they meant at first. I was like 18 or 19, an Italian girl from a good Catholic family. Two days later it hits me, and I go, "Oh my goodness!" I go into work, and I pointed around the room and asked, "What about her?

What about her?" And they said, "Exactly." I wanted to be a broker, but not that way.

Melanie Griffith could have based her character in *Working Girl* on me; I was *that* determined.

Yet with all this studying and hard work, I was still held back—because I was a woman. There were many women in the business who were smarter, worked harder, and still would not become a broker or make equal pay. The salaries were not even close. How about getting "let go" or fired as a female employee? Many times, no one knew why or they knew not to ask.

As you will see, women could be fired or demoted for just about anything—or for nothing, really.

I gradually moved up in the departments. I started in the government agency department, which then moved across the hall and I was asked to stay and work on the 2-year and 5-year note desk, which is a step up. Not much later it was requested I move to the long bond desk. The long bond and the bond market are still spoken about on CNN, CNBC and other news networks, and is mentioned in the *Wall Street Journal* and the New York *Times*.

When I wasn't at work, I loved shopping and used my new salary to go out and buy clothes or have some custom made that were suitable for my new position in life. I was also able to help out my mother. She wouldn't accept rent, but she would let me buy groceries. I was able to fly out to the west coast to visit family, and I really enjoyed traveling to spas for self-care and some R & R.

A good deal of my time was spent on traveling to and from work. When I started, I took the train from Brooklyn to Manhattan. After I became a broker, I requested more money so I could move to the city since all my clients lived there, and the commute home was exhausting after entertaining clients late into the evening and on weekends.

I was enjoying life very much. I had many friends both male and female who I worked with and a few of my clients became friends, too. We went to sporting events, wine school, Broadway shows, concerts, and enjoyed fine dining at landmarks like Le Bernadin, The 21 Club, Windows on the World, and more. I especially enjoyed the museums and going out dancing.

I worked as an assistant and also unofficially picked up the phones (52 accounts calling to get in on a trade) and I brokered any chance I could, mostly when no one could pick up the important accounts. I loved it and really wanted to be a broker. Jumping in to pick up the accounts (clients) was not always fun. They'd be upset that their broker was not attending to them. They'd yell and curse as they would give their order. Buy this, sell that, (the Long Bond, etc.) or if they were pissed off they'd say, "Take me out of everything!"

The head of my department was something else. He thought he was a god. Don't get me wrong, he was a nice-looking man, well dressed, smelled good, but who didn't back then?

You remember Michael Douglas in *Wall Street* and Leonardo DiCaprio in *The Wolf of Wall Street*? My boss looked like them and his head could just barely fit through the doorway because his ego was sadly so big. He was fun and funny and also inappropriate most of the time. He was known to ask the color and size of the women's nipples, tossing a quarter and half dollars telling us ladies to measure and let him know which matched yours best. He was married and also had a steady girlfriend who I think he had children with.

I remember one time I got up to go get coffee and as I walked past the trading desk, one of the brokers threw (well made it look like he dropped) pencils on the floor in front of me hoping I would bend over so he could see up my skirt. As I went to retrieve the pencils, he then tried to stop me. I said, "I got them," and bent my knees as I was taught at home and in Catholic school. I smiled and said. "Here you go," and walked away. I guess he hoped I'd be stupid enough to just bend over for him.

I was working in the bond department where the high rollers played. Like in the movies, we had carte blanche. Our department brought in the most money, so we could get away with almost anything. The company had on-staff chefs since we could not leave the trading floor except to use the restroom or grab a coffee. Most things were brought to us so we could stay focused. Our boss would order food a couple of days a week, either Japanese or Italian. He would also order in wine. Why not? He was Leonardo DiCaprio; at least that is what he and his ego thought.

Our boss would tell the ticket writers to go to the bank and get $100 bills exchanged into singles. He would say, "Let's watch the rats chase the money like cheese." He was referring to the people outside as though they were beneath him, no more than rats that roamed the streets. He would then open the third-floor window and throw the dollar bills out and watch them flitter to the street below. He'd have the other men stand by the opened windows, yelling out and laughing. Until one day, the NYC police came up and gave the department a warning.

He would also grab or touch some of the girls' asses when they walked by. That did not happen to me, thank God. I thought maybe he had some integrity ... until one night.

I was heading out the door, many of the guys said, "Maria, we are all going out and Sam wants you to join us."

I joined the department for what I thought was a quick dinner in New York, but we ended up back in the boss' neighborhood in New Jersey. Sam took us to a place he called "Bar A." He kept touching my leg, my knee. I thought "Oh, no." I threw my head back smiling and would move his hand, hoping he would stop. He did not. I thought "he's drunk," and "I can't blame him for trying." I smiled and continued to move his hand off over and over, in the most polite way possible. Thinking back now, I was so young. Why the hell was I so polite? I was exhausted from the night and the effort to fend him off, and finally, I was able to get a car home. Never could I have imagined what happened next.

When I arrived at work the next morning, one of the men who was out with us asked to speak with me. I followed him to the back of the room, where he asked me to sit down. He tells me they have to let me go.

"Let me go?! What for?" I ask.

All he would say was to leave quietly. In shock, I grabbed my things and start walking out and the same feeling came over me that I had in junior high school when that boy grabbed me. Something about this whole situation didn't feel right.

Listen, it was a man's world and as I was seeing it, I had three choices: 1) Leave with my tail between my legs and not get hired anywhere since I was "fired." 2) Sue them, which really never crossed my mind because I would be blackballed and not hired in the industry. Or 3) Do what I *felt* I needed to do. I chose Option 3.

I went to the office of the man who hired me, Vinny, the president of the company.

I ask to see Vinny and waited. The man who told me I was fired saw me there when he was on his way to the men's room. He stopped and told me once again that I better go. I stand up, nervous on the inside, and said, "Vinny hired me, and he will have to be the man who fires me."

The man got red in the face and ran back to his desk. The phone rings at Vinny's secretary's desk. She puts the call through, and then Vinny called me into his office.

It's like walking into Gordon Gekko's office. I liked the feeling of being in his office, his power to keep me on or to let me go. Vinny had the power over that man whose ego was hurt and wanted to punish me.

Vinny says, "I heard what happened."

I asked Vinny if he would allow me to tell my side of the story. As I began to speak, he looks shocked and a little bit scared, or maybe he was upset that they just called him and told him lies regarding me. He says, "Maria, please don't worry. You are not fired. Take the company car, go shopping, go home and relax, and come back Monday morning. I'll have this all straightened out."

It was then that I realized he feared I would sue them. I would never, if I wanted to work on Wall Street. I would have been blackballed.

Had I not chosen Option 3, I would not have had a career. This treatment of women was pervasive and is still happening today. We get to stand as women in grace, and I am truly grateful for all the women who have stood up, not just for themselves, but are the pioneers for women's rights. This is why it is so important to document everything. Whether you decide to take action on it when it happens, at a later date, or never. That documentation will serve you well.

I was moved back to the Agency department where we brokered Fannie Mae, Freddie Mac and home loans. I had started with them, had a few friends there, and was treated pretty well for a woman.

I later told a few close friends about the incident. At that time, it was the norm to be treated that way. I felt lucky to be invited into the club and understood that staying there was contingent on knowing my place. The whole thing was kept very hush hush.

I never became a broker at Fundamental Brokers. My friend Ann worked for RMJ securities and suggested I apply there. So that is what I did. They were a wonderful firm and did say that they would make me a broker. I felt heard and respected there.

It was at RMJ that I was approached to interview for a broker position at a company adding a government agency department. They had heard a lot about me. The owners of RMJ securities were a class act and I believe at some point I would have become a broker there. It was the department heads and the other male brokers who just were not ready to allow a woman to compete with them on the trading floor.

It was odd - I interviewed with two men, one was trying hard to recruit me and the other was trying to scare me off, it seemed. I didn't think anything of it at the time. I told them what I was making and why I wanted to move with them to start up this department. The one said, "Well you don't have any accounts." To which I replied, "I do," and gave him the name. He proceeded to make light of it.

I assure you if I were a man, I would have gotten a much higher salary than I requested. They agreed to give me more money, but not the full amount I had put on the table. So, I asked, "If I prove myself in six months, will you give me what I am requesting?" They did not think I would do as well as I stated, so they agreed. I had them put it in writing. This is my advice to everyone; don't be afraid to say, "Let's put this in writing."

I started each day by asking my clients to paint pictures. This is a term used when putting in a bid lower than what most are bidding and an offer higher than what most are selling at. Other traders would then come in and put the bids and offerings where they should be. This would then create trades and business for us. It was very helpful since we were the new guys.

By the age of 26, I became the only female broker in the government agency department for Garban, which brokered Fannie Mae and Freddie Mac home loans. By age 26, I was making six figures.

I was feeling proud. Deep down I knew I could accomplish anything I wanted, but all those "**you'll nevers**" were still in my head. I heard a voice say those words to me so many times, as if it were wrong of me to be here. The feeling I had would go up and down depending on who I was with. I would get nervous and have a feeling of unease (more like dis-ease) when I went places where my father and his wife would be. I felt sick, unworthy, and knew something demeaning would be said to me. How would I handle it?

My way of bolstering myself was to put on my armor. I would read the word of God from a little and very powerful book every morning: *God's Creative Power Will Work for You*, by Charles Capps. It is the size of a small cell phone, so it was easy to keep with me.

I would also go in my closet and pick out something to wear that would make me feel good. I know this may sound silly, yet I felt like I had to gear myself up to be in a room with my father and his wife. There were many, many a time I was hurt by the words of my father and more by the things his wife would say to me.

Reading from *God's Creative Power*, and wearing my nice clothing somehow made me know I made it and was worthy. Whether at my sister's or an event, my father's wife would catch me alone and intentionally harass me.

When my goddaughter was baptized, my company sent me to the event in a white limo. That gesture made me feel like I had finally made it. After the baptism, we were back at my sister's house where I was helping in the kitchen. My father's wife comes in bragging very loudly about her daughter being a teacher and the salary she is making. I hold back comment, knowing what I make at that time far exceeded that amount, and of course I have no student loans. She goes on and on. Then looks over at me and says, "Well Maria, aren't you lucky to have gotten your job?" She never says the title of my position. I feel sick inside. It hurts, and no one like my sister, brother-in-law, or mother were nearby to hear her.

I pushed out a smile and said calmly, "Yes. I was lucky to get the job and it is not luck that keeps me there. I clearly proved I belong." I was hurt, but I swept my hair across my shoulder and walked away with my head held high.

Another time, I have to attend a family wedding. I do not want to go alone since I know she will be there, so I invite my friend George to be my plus one. He's such a class act. We are sitting with my sister during the entree portion of the wedding, when my father's wife walks over. Now we know she does not care for me. She sits on my chair and practically pushes me off. My sister is next to me as my father's wife starts telling us a story of when she was a little girl. I'm wondering, "Where is this going?" She says her mom bought her a coat one winter. It was a nice coat, but she would not wear it. When her mother asked why, she tells us, "I told my mother, it's RED! And you know, mom, red brings too much attention to you."

She looks at me and says, "That's why you wear it, right Maria?"

Well, you know what color dress I had on. Yes RED. My sister was there for the first time to witness this woman's cutting verbal attack. I again smile, hurt and feeling bad, not feeling worthy, and still I spoke. "Don't be silly. People would pay attention to me no matter what color I wore." She seemed annoyed at my confident and quick comeback and walked away.

There was another time I was at a charity event with my family. It was outside on a very large property. After some time, I excused myself to use the ladies' room, which because it was an outside venue meant using a porta potty. Well, I went in and when I came out there were people there, with cameras, taking photos of me. It was my father's wife and her daughter, laughing and laughing at me. His wife said, "I bet you never expected that! To have pictures of you leaving a porta potty."

Ugh these people, if that's what we should refer to them as. I replied, "I absolutely would expect it from you," and walked back to my seat.

It finally came to me that some people do not want to rise or that maybe they think they can rise by hurting others or by trying to tear them down. I was not going to stoop down to her level, but instead rise higher. I want to set a good example for my children.

It was after that episode, at almost 40 years old, that I spoke with my dad and said, "I love you, and you may come to see the children and me anytime. I will no longer be treated poorly by your wife or allow that language or behavior near my children."

Respect does not have to be given; it is earned. I was raised to respect others, but I questioned what if those in charge, who should know better, are not doing better for those who look to them? Do young children have to follow the rules if they are in danger, or should we teach children and women to take a stand in grace and in honor of themselves? When those "in charge" break the rules, what are we to teach? I taught my children if someone says, "Do not tell your parents," to say, "Okay, of course not." Then when they are safe or with their dad or me, tell us. I told them that we will care for them. I reminded them, "The only one who can take care of you is you when we are not there."

When I arrived at these events, I would just smile because I understood that I really didn't need anyone else to believe in me. I only needed to believe in myself.

Belief in myself led me to I apply to another brokerage firm, RMJ Securities, down the Street, at One Seaport Plaza.

I was hired, loved it there, and learned a lot. The president and vice-president were very nice.

We were all treated very well, and I stayed there for a couple of years.

Then I was contacted by four men who were starting up the Government Agencies Department at one of the top brokerage houses on the street. They had been given my name. On Wall Street most interviews and talks are done quietly. If you do decide to leave the firm you are with for another one, you must leave as soon as possible. They basically escort you out of the building.

I had a breakfast interview at the famous Delmonico's with two men from Garban, one they called Cop, since he was a former officer, and the other, Donny.

I mentioned to my mom that I was being recruited by another company. She said, "Why would you leave, Maria? They treat you well."

I said, "Yes, and I still want to be a broker. This company will give me that opportunity, plus I can ask for more."

"Maria, you are asking for more? How can you do that?"

"Mom, it is what is usually done, and I will have a lot more responsibility and time that is required."

She felt that I was taking a chance and was not really in agreement with me, or maybe feared it would not work out for me.

I decided to take this opportunity since they offered me a broker position, and not just a broker, the only female broker in the department. I turned the **you'll never** into **I can**, **I will**, and **I did**.

I had four bosses and got along with all of them, except Donny. He did not seem very fond of me, or any woman for that matter. He always had a comment, "What are you going to do with those long nails? How will you type?" I answered, "I will cut them."

"What about your commute?"

"What about it? I mean, so many of us have long commutes."

I started doing well and was given an account by a co-worker, Brian, who was heading off to our London office. He gave me Rothschild & Co. and I covered two of the traders from that company. I had my friend and client at Yamaichi and three other accounts.

I was in this department with 13 men, four of them were my bosses, and no one told me that my two accounts, Yamaichi and Rothschild, were in the top five every month since we opened.

What?! I had no idea. Donny had me move to sit next to him. He wanted to keep an eye on me, and apparently, an ear, too. The comments kept coming and I knew I had to let them go. After all, I was lucky to be invited, remember?

One day, it was a 29 lock on the Long Home Loan. A lock means that a buyer and a seller agree to the price or that is how it looks on the computer screen. A lock usually means a trade will occur. It is the person (account) that initiates the trade that pays us the commission. At that time in the '80s I believe we received $32 a million. I know it does not seem like much, until you do a trade of 50, 100, 250 million dollars. Out of respect for my fellow brokers, I call each client even if I know they do not trade the long end of the market. Why? It is what we should do, and you never know if your client needs to hedge himself or if an underwriter throws something at him. Most traders get annoyed when you bother them, so I had a code, a saying so they would not get upset. I'd say, "Just so you know."

That day I said, "Just so you know, there's a 29 lock on the Long Home Loan."

Donny, who has been listening to me on the phone, yells angrily, "Why do you always say that?!"

I smiled and said. "Well, I guess it is working for me." He turned red and stormed off.

I was nervous about my response to Donny until all the men stood up and clapped. Yes, they started clapping, and said, "It's about time you stood up to him, Maria."

"But he is so upset …"

"Don't you know, Maria?"

"Know what?"

"You Maria, are the number one broker in this department."

I was so proud and excited. The bosses had never shown me the numbers. Of course, they didn't tell me. Although I was not making what I should, I was happy to have the support of my male counterparts.

Our department was moved up one floor where more of the action was now that we had proven ourselves. We were located right next to T-bills which stands for treasury bills - 3-month, 6-month, etc.

It was then that my client and friend from Yamaichi announced he was leaving the company. His assistant called me and said he wanted to talk with me. Would I be available to meet him after work? I said, "Sure, let's grab a bite and talk."

He told me, "Since Ken is going, all the brokerage firms are putting me with brokers I do not know, and since you helped me a lot when I started, I was wondering if you too were passing me along."

"Don't be silly. It never crossed my mind."

He said, "I was told another guy I do not know in your department will be covering me."

I was shocked but would not let him know it.

The rule has always been "what the customer wants the customer gets." Plus, this was my account. I went into the office the next day and I tell Donny my client will be calling in, as he has asked if I would continue as his broker since I have been with him from the beginning.

It was before the market opened and Donny was reading the newspaper. He snapped it sharply, looked at me, and said, "So yesterday he seemed fine with the idea, and now you have 'dinner' with him, and he changes his mind."

I said, "What?! What are you insinuating?"

Donny answered, "I am not insinuating; I am telling you…"

"Telling me what? That I slept with him? That's crazy."

He stops talking and turns his back to me. I say, "I need this like I need a hole in the head. I have not only proven myself; I am the top broker in our department!" I was furious and walked straight to the VP's office.

The VP listened to me and told me he'd have a meeting later that day. True to his word, at the end of the business day, the VP calls the four bosses and me into a small room. The other three bosses have no idea what Donny accused me of. They look shocked and Donny decides to deny saying it, "Well that's not good."

I go over it until, finally, Donny admits what he said to me. At that moment all the men know what this means and what could happen if word gets out. The VP asks me to leave the room. I was not happy about that, but I left as asked.

After some time, they come out of the room and the VP comes over to me. He says, "Everything is fine. Come in tomorrow and we will have this all straightened out." He tells me Donny is sorry. Yet I never hear Donny say it.

For the next week or so, things seem different as I go through my day, although I am still sitting next to Donny. He hears me on the phone with my friend and former client from Yamaichi and tells me I can't talk to him that way. I reply that he is also a friend and I am trying to help him.

I end up helping my friend from Yamaichi get placed at another company making more money, and it was the way I spoke with my former client and friend that helped him realize he needed to be interviewing.

I thought everything was back to normal when the VP called me into his office. "Maria the Ginnie Mae desk needs help, and I was thinking you could help them out for a while."

Hmmm … that's interesting. I wasn't sure about this move but did not think I had a choice. He said, "Maria, this will be good for you."

It did seem good at first. The head of the Ginnie Mae department was very nice. We worked together to determine which accounts I would cover and what I could help with. They even allowed me to go to Windows on The World Wine School with my new client. There, I learned a lot while having fun.

A short time later, my new boss came to me and said, "Maria I don't think our department can afford your salary."

"Really?" I replied. "Didn't the VP tell you?"

"Tell me what?" he asked.

"I am under contract and my salary cannot be lowered."

It was clear what was happening and months later the VP calls me in to his office and says, "Maria, let's get you a job. We need to place you before your contract is up. I want to help you. I wish you could have swallowed your pride and just let what Donny said to you go."

I sat up in my chair, in my late 20s, and said, "Someday, I may have a daughter and I don't want her to have to swallow her pride out of fear."

Looking back, I realize that while Donny was very wrong, maybe being right is not always right. (I made this a saying now.) Learning to let things go may be helpful. I think I was tired of all nonsense the women had to go through and felt that someone needed to take a stand. That stand cost me a $30,000 bonus. None of this would have happened had I been a man.

I headed off to Liberty Brokers with the help of Garban's VP, working on the 7- and 10-year desk covering Drexel Burnham Lambert and a few other accounts.

At Liberty, I sat next to a man who had been in the business for years, a veteran who had incredible clients and friends. We helped each other out and I learned a lot from him. I was able to type very fast and would help him with that and back him up on all of his accounts.

It was fun and I saw a lot. Things that were similar to movies about Wall Street. "Working in the gray area," as the guys would say. "It's fine."

Well I don't think the Securities and Exchange Commission would think so.

77 Water Street.
New York NY 10005
212 574 1776

**Liberty
Brokerage
Inc.**

September 26, 1988

Maria Forte
196 West 10th Street
New York, New York 10014

Maria:

I am pleased you made the decision to join us at Liberty. We look forward to working with you; and I am sure you will find this a rewarding and professional career opportunity.

You will be a Broker at Liberty Brokerage Inc. starting Monday, September 26, 1988 at an annual salary of $65,000 and an opportunity for an additional incentive compensation award based on your performance and the financial circumstances of Liberty.

Maria, this letter is not to be construed as an employment contract. We look forward to you joining us and would appreciate it if you would confirm the above as the basis of your employment.

Sincerely,

Thomas M. Wendel
President and
Chief Executive Officer

Confirmed: _____
              Maria Forte

Broker at Liberty Brokerage

The new boss in my department came over from the FBI long bond desk—the same place where I was nearly fired for not sleeping with the boss. He was there a short time before he started putting fake bids and offerings on the screen. This means that there is not an investor or a bank that called this order in, no trader, no underwriter. We are a brokerage firm and we do not have the authority to take position in the market.

Then this new boss started hitting the bids and offerings showing we had a trade. Again, not legal. The department became quiet while they watched him do this. Then many of the men began to yell, "What are you doing? We can't do this."

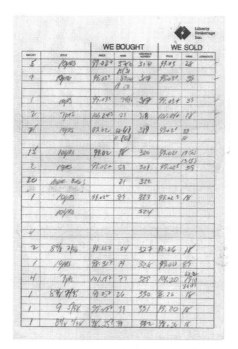

Broker notes at Liberty Brokerage

Broker Buy and Sell tickets

"Calm down," he'd say. "We will take ourselves out once the traders come in." Remember I said to document things at your office, even if they may seem little.

This new boss who took me aside when he first arrived, saying he had my back and would take care of me and all in our department, telling me he's here to turn this department around—well he didn't say how ...

I realized that I did not want to make money this way and be a part of this. I loved being a broker and the lifestyle that came with it. I started to feel I should make a plan B. Maybe my zeal was not the same. Maybe others noticed.

One late Friday afternoon when I was ready to head home, one of the VPs and one of my department heads asked to speak with me. It was last-minute and I had an appointment. I said, "Of course," and I also told them I would not be able to stay long. "It won't take long," they assured me.

They went on to tell me the income flow of the department and that I would have to bring in more. I said, "Great, the trader for Lehman Brothers asked if I would cover her when I took over for my co-worker (her broker) while he went on vacation." This kind of thing happens. It has happened to me. Sometimes the trader and broker click and flow better.

They said, "We can't do that." Interesting since it's done all the time, and I thought to myself, "What else can I do to generate more business?" Each time I mentioned something they turned it down. "Okay," I said. "This is like a carpenter whose tools have been taken away. How can I do my job if you will not give me my tools?"

This went on and on until I said, "Let's pick this up on Monday once we have a chance to digest this information. Plus, I do have an appointment." "Maria, if you leave, don't bother coming back."

"What?! I don't mean any disrespect. This was not planned, or I assure you I would have moved things around." We spoke some more going around in an exhausting circle. Finally, I said, "I am sorry, but I must make my appointment."

They yelled, "Then you're fired!"

What a way to go, and really that was the way they planned it to go from the start.

I had a quiet weekend and the next week I was advised to go to the unemployment office. It was strange experience for me; I had never been there before. I filled out what I needed to and waited to be called. I was due to get the maximum amount of money. The woman asked me questions, wrote things down, and told me I'll have to step away while she calls my employer. I waited as I was told.

She finally calls me back to her desk and says, "I am sorry; you won't be able to collect because you were let go because of insubordination."

I said confidently, "Really?" and I whip out my calendar book. Yes, I referred to the notes I had taken. I asked, "Was I insubordinate when I did not sit on the boss's lap on this day?" as I pointed to a date in the calendar book. "Was I insubordinate when . . .? Was I on this date? Was I . . .?"

She calmly responded, "Please wait, as I have to call them back."

In a few minutes, she called me over to her little booth and said, "You will be receiving the full amount due you, and it is because they, your former employer could not comment on one date or one thing I challenged them on from your documentation."

I thanked her and she gave me an understanding look and a good feeling. I walked out thinking, "Wow, advocating for myself in this arena of men has taught me more than I imagined." I look back now and I am very grateful for it all.

Lessons Learned. Getting my foot in the door is only the first step. It is up to me to learn what I need to get ahead. Life isn't fair for women in a male-dominated business, but I do not need to compromise my goals or my values to achieve my dreams. When I stand up for myself, I am standing up for countless other women.

Chapter 4. The Greatest Salesman Ever

Marriage and Divorce

"Salespeople have one of the hardest jobs in the world to do. They deal with rejection on a daily basis. Making a sale comes down to powering through call after call, e-mail after e-mail and no after no."

—Brian Tracy

In 1989 I left Wall Street and moved to Florida for a year. That was my plan B. My cousin Carmela and her family lived in Florida, and we spoke almost every day. Since I always enjoyed visiting with her, her husband Frank and other family there, I thought, "Why not move to Florida?"

After the pace and intensity of the New York life, I was relaxing for a while. I moved in with Carmela, Frank, their new baby, Lorenzo, and dog Rocky.

I was offered a job in Miami, and the pay was less than what I was making at age 18. It was not enough to afford my lifestyle. I was trying to decide whether to go back to Wall Street or maybe help my cousin Susan who was in the music business in Los Angeles.

Susan was the vice president of Casablanca Records. My aunt Tina had six daughters and Susan was the oldest of the six. We all grew up together and she was a big support to me when my mom was ill. When Susan moved to LA, my aunt along with my cousins were not far behind. I missed them and would visit often. My cousin Toniann and I were closest in age and hung out very often. She would work at Susan's office, which meant I would go to the office to see her when I visited California.

It was very cool to have my aunt Tina have us help with dinner no matter who was coming over. That's what we always did. Cut, chop dice, put pasta on, etc.

On one of my visits, Susan asked what I was planning next. She told me I could help work with her if I wanted to move to LA. I gave it great thought. My mother and sister were on the East Coast, as were many of my friends. I really appreciated Susan's offer, but decided to stay on the East Coast.

Before leaving California, I went to visit cousin Tommy who was a musician. He said, "Oh, if you end up back in New York or in the New York area, you should give my friend a call." A few months later, I did wind up back in New York and I agreed to meet his friend, the man who would become my husband.

Tommy's friend, Soapy, called me several times over the next month. We would talk a little bit on the phone, and he would ask me out every time. But I really wasn't interested at first, but after a few months I finally agreed to go out with him.

Tommy had sent Soapy a picture of me, and when he came to the door, he said, "You look just like I pictured." I responded, "You look nothing like I pictured." I had pictured someone who looked Italian since every time we spoke he told me he and his family are just like Italians. His mom cooked Italian, he loved Italians and his friends are Italian.

Soapy took me on a date in New York and it went pretty well. We went to The Grand Ticino in the West Village. It's the same restaurant featured in the movie *Moonstruck*. He was extremely charming and continued to contact me and ask me out.

I was hesitant to go out with him again; he lived far away, but he just continued the pursuit. The way he pursued me seemed attractive. He would drive to New York from his place in New Jersey, take me out to dinner, and then drive home.

We started dating regularly and he told me that he occasionally smoked cigarettes. I told him, "I can't handle smoke. I don't smoke." He responded, "Oh yeah, your cousin told me."

I later found out that he told his family he actually couldn't afford to take me out. He knew that I worked on Wall Street. I did very well for myself, so I guess he was trying to impress me. It worked. I wish he told me up front and not kept these important facts from me.

When we first started seeing each other, I loved dating him. He was fun. He could be extremely funny. He had a very good personality.

When we ran into people who knew him, they would talk about what a great musician he was, and what a great drummer he was. Although, I've never known him for that.

I was travelling back and forth from Florida to New York for a bit and was looking to find a place there because I started working for a friend of mine who owned Royal Windows. I was doing sales for him, and it wasn't really the ideal thing. He allowed me to live in the apartment above the office until I found my own place.

Soapy asked me, "Why don't you move to New Jersey? Why don't you move in with me?" I had never moved in with anyone that I was dating before, but decided to move in with him to see how it would go.

I lived with Soapy for a few weeks. It felt strange and I could not put my finger on what was going on, so I left and moved in with my sister in New Jersey. He then took me out one night and said he was dealing with something and felt we should not date. We broke up and I found out later that he was using drugs.

We still talked. I had never known anyone personally with a drug problem before and did not know how to recognize the signs. He would go out and come home shortly after and be exhausted, then go right to sleep. I'd be like, "Oh my God, I don't get it. What's going on?" He was very thin and in shape.

A few months later, Soapy called me one day at my sister's in the middle of a snowstorm and told me, "I'm really sick. I have the flu. Can you help me?" I cooked some food for him and grabbed some sheets from my sister's house. I drove through the snow to get to his place. I stayed for two or three days, taking care of him and slept on the couch while he was in his room. When he got better, he confessed to me that he had a drug problem.

I decided to set up an intervention. He has three brothers and a sister, who didn't really want anything to do with him at that time. I think they were so disappointed. But his one brother, came to meet Soapy and me while I was at a friend's house helping watch her children. He started talking to me and he said, "We've already tried this. Been there. Done that. It's not going to help. Run as fast as you can." Nobody really supported him.

I went to Soapy and said, "Listen, if your family isn't going to help you, you have got to help yourself. Call your company. They can't fire you. I said, "Call your human resources and see if you can get help."

HR did help him, as it was part of their medical coverage. After this, I started driving him to Red Bank, New Jersey, for appointments and recovery meetings elsewhere.

I completely supported him during that time, and once in a while I would take him to his meetings and wait outside for him. He seemed to be getting better and started working again. To me, he seemed humbled by the experience and was grateful that I helped him. Going through that experience together made me feel closer to him and we got together intimately.

Pretty quickly, I had an idea I may be pregnant and took a home pregnancy test. It showed positive, so I went to a doctor to confirm it. I told Soapy and explained I would be fine and would get help to care for the baby on my own. He said, "Don't be silly."

When I was three months pregnant with my son, the doctor told me she discovered cervical cancer. I had to have a procedure and Soapy was there with me for that. I was going through drug rehabilitation with him; and now he was going through this with me, strengthening the ties between us.

It was a very scary time. I did not want to lose my child and was concerned. Maybe I would not be able to have children after this. It was during that time that Soapy suggested we get married. At first, I said, "No, I'm going to take care of this myself."

At the hospital I told them that my medical coverage had ended, and they directed me to where I could apply for assistance with social services. Yes, I needed financial help and it was a good thing, since I had medical difficulties with that pregnancy. I ended up on what they call WIC. I was able to get the medical care I needed at that time, food to nourish me, and care for my son for a year after his birth. Since his father had been on drugs, I was concerned for my son's overall health; we both were.

When I told social services that Soapy had been on drugs, they were concerned for my unborn child, and they said, "When the child is born, we will come to the house." Consequently, they came to the house quite often to make sure our son's development was not affected. I guess they did that for a year or a little bit more.

Soapy asked me to marry him again, and I said yes, thinking this might be best for both of us. At the time, Soapy was living in a garage apartment, drove a Pontiac, and was making very little money, maybe $30,000 a year. In the state of New Jersey, that's not a lot. I saw something in him that I don't think others saw. I put aside his past and started to envision our future together.

We got married on Saturday October 12, 1991, and the next day we drove to the Poconos. On the way there, Soapy continually pulled to the side of the road to smoke and place bets from a pay phone. Every chance he got he pulled over. I can't even count the number of times he pulled over. When we finally got to our hotel, he kept the TV on, and I was pregnant, and he was smoking, and he was gambling and obviously back on the drugs. His behavior scared me. I didn't know if it was my hormones making me feel this way. I also wondered if this was how life was going to be for us from now on.

On the way home I was extremely quiet, and he looked over at me and said, "I sold you. I sold you." And that's why I say he is the greatest salesman ever. He could be as charming and convincing as can be. And he certainly did sell me on marrying him.

I thought we would stay in his garage apartment, but he said, "No, no, no," and we rented a townhome in Brick, New Jersey. It wasn't very nice. Everybody lent us furniture, and nothing matched. We had a mattress on the floor until Soapy's aunt and uncle bought us a bed. We both decided that I would stay home with the baby because neither one of us had our mom at home growing up. I think that was the only thing that we agreed upon.

Coming from Wall Street, being very independent, loving to shop, and being used to really nice clothing, this new life was going to be an adjustment. But I was committed to it and I was committed to my family. I decided I wasn't going to buy anything; we would focus our resources on raising this child. We did, and for a while everything seemed fine. The first year was rocky, but seemed to start turning around when Soapy began focusing more on work and his income increased.

Soapy had some relapses and it was difficult for me. Our son got older and we were still in the townhome when I got pregnant with our second child, a daughter. We then decided that we were going to buy our first home. We had a little saved and we knew this was what we wanted. We borrowed from each of our parents. Four thousand from his father and four thousand from my mother. We paid them both back over time and it felt good to be able to do that.

One day, when I was pregnant with our daughter, I came home from the grocery store and was putting the groceries away in the pantry, when all of a sudden Soapy pushed me. He pushed me so hard I fell through the kitchen wall. My son, just a toddler, was standing there and saw all this. It knocked the wind out of me, and Soapy saw the look on our son's face. Was it the drugs that made him do that? I don't know.

When Soapy realized what he did, he was so remorseful. "Maria, this will never happen again. I will never do this again." But he was always confrontational. He's a bully. He told me he had always been a bully.

I'm not working, I'm pregnant with my second child and we were buying a home. And I'm thinking, well, what am I going to do now? I was living in an area that I didn't know. I mean, I'm from New York, my mom is in New York, my cousins, my family, but this situation was not something I was used to.

The first place I sought help was at Providence House in Toms River, New Jersey. When they interviewed me, they showed me a sketch of a person's body and asked me to mark on there where I was ever hit or bruised.

I discovered 180 Turning Lives Around. They showed me film clips about domestic abuse and asked, "Can you relate to any of these?" On different days I could relate to each of them.

The children witnessed my abuse, whether they still remember it or not it is in their subconscious. Soapy never physically abused them, thankfully, but he was unquestionably verbally abusive, which is, of course, emotionally abusive.

The children witnessed some of the physical abuse, but it wasn't apparent to other people. Once my husband's career took off, people would see me in a nice home and think I saw myself as a princess. Many would ask "What does your husband do?" I'd smile and say, "He sells soap."

We built Soapy's career together. I did not go back to work and I don't have any regrets about that. That was probably one of the only things we agreed upon—that I would stay at home with our children. I am still very grateful for that and thankful to him. It shows in our children.

I was prepared to sacrifice—not shopping, not doing this, not doing that. There were times Soapy told me, "**you'll never**." You can't go by this; you can't do that. You can't." That life was quite restrictive for us. I couldn't do things for the children, like buying clothes for them without first having to ask. I felt like a kid, not a grown woman. There was one time Soapy actually forbade me to buy clothing for my children. He said we didn't have the money. And our children didn't have clothes that fit, and I was going to do something about it.

My daughter was still under a year old, and my son was three at the time. I looked around my living room and noticed the curtains. They were custom ordered from JCPenney. I dragged a chair in from the dining room, and took those curtains right off the rods, leaving only the sheers over the windows. I folded them up and returned them to the store. The store clerk gave me $250 for them and I walked right to the children's department to buy my children what they needed.

I knew I was going to be in big trouble when Soapy got home. He walked in and noticed the curtains were gone, so I said, "Well, we don't have the money and the children need clothes, so I had to get creative."

A turning point came on a Monday night in November. I asked Soapy, "Can you watch the kids? I'm going to go to the grocery store." And he said, "Yeah, but don't spend more than $60." The total came to $62 and change. I came home and started to put the groceries away when he came into the kitchen and demanded to see the receipt. He flipped out because I spent $2 more than he said, and he knocked me into the refrigerator.

I sat on the floor for what seemed like a half an hour to me, but it was probably just a minute, because I was afraid Soapy would hit me again. He had left marks on my arm and marks on my face. I got scared and ran upstairs and grabbed my kids and went into the master bedroom and locked the door. I called my sister and then called the police. I felt sick to my stomach, scared, and so confused.

When the police came, the officer told me that I didn't need to file charges. (That officer was later fired.) I was in duress and wasn't thinking clearly. My in-laws came over a few days later and were talking a lot. They told me, "You don't want to have a problem come the holidays. You don't want this. You don't want that. Are you pressing charges?"

I said, "I don't think I need to." It wasn't that I didn't have enough sense. All the drama and the chatter were swirling around me. This is why it is so important to have the right people around you. You need people who will protect you. My in-laws didn't protect me. They put me back into the fire and I still have a hard time forgetting that. It is so difficult to understand they were not thinking of my children or me and our wellbeing. It was really more about them and not about protecting another human being.

It was the county that pressed charges as part of its domestic violence procedure. I went to court and stood up to testify about what happened that night. The judge asked if they should drop the charges and I saw this as an opportunity to have something good come out of a horrific situation. I responded, "Not unless he's forced to go for help." The judge said to him "It's a good idea and I will need a report. You will go for counseling," he told him. Although Soapy went for help, we were instructed to go to counseling together. That didn't work out at all. It was just all fluff. And then the behavior started again. Looking back, it made no sense to have couple's counseling when I could not express myself. But I wanted to in hopes it would keep our family together.

That whole experience reinforced for me that Soapy had an addictive personality. He was also a gambler. When he would lose, which is what happened on that Monday night, he found out what he owed the bookie from the Sunday or Monday night games and he took it out on me. It really wasn't about me. The $2 and change. I mean who cares? Some people might say, "Well, what'd you do to get him upset?" I don't want any other woman to ever feel like there's something they did.

I stayed with him because I had made a commitment to stay home with our children and help him with his career. He would tell me, "I want to be like Tim." Tim was one of the top salesmen for the company; Joe from Detroit was number one. We would go to the company sales meetings and Tim would be sitting at the podium with the head honchos—the President, VP, etc. Soapy would point to him and say, "Wow that Tim. If I could just do half of what he does I'd be happy." And I asked him, "What do you mean?"

"Look at him up on the podium." And I said, "Why can't you do better than him? Why don't we have Tim and his family for dinner or go out with them. Maybe he'll help you. You're not in the same territory." We became very close to them. They are a wonderful family and our children all got along very well.

We became a partnership because I took care of everything: the children, the home, the cooking, the cleaning, etc., etc. All he had to do was roll out of bed and go sell, not always easy but he was great at it. I made a lot of suggestions. When we were first together, he would say I was beautiful, and I was intelligent. When he needed my help he would say, "She's so smart." "What do you think of this?" He would run things by me. I enjoyed that because I was used to that with different people in my life, in my career.

Tim did help Soapy. He taught him the car wash industry. Soapy ended up in the million-dollar club. He became the number one salesman in his company while we were married. He went from almost zero to that. The company gave him many awards and for me a pen and a pair of beautiful diamond earrings. They asked me to give a speech at the dinner where Soapy was recognized. I told a story about when he was a drummer. I said, "I didn't know him then. Thank God he became a salesman." I was proud of Soapy, but I didn't realize that money is like alcohol. Money makes you more of who you really are.

When Soapy started to make more money, he started putting me down and wanted me to feel "less than." It made him feel like King Kong or Godzilla to do that, and he just no longer needed my help. I was insignificant to him at that point and he did not value me.

I changed through the process because I was hurt that he didn't value me anymore. We began as a partnership. He now tells my son that we had nothing. "Your mom went to Kmart and she'd put together these cardboard things that turned into drawers. It's like disposable furniture. And we lived with that for a while. We had a bed on the floor."

Then all of a sudden, we build this big, beautiful stucco home. My dream since childhood has been to have a beautiful home where I could entertain. We had many people over to show our home. It was wonderful. The children loved having lots of people over. Then things changed, I changed, and it was no longer what I envisioned. Soapy no longer wanted to entertain.

When Soapy became very successful, he decided he no longer needed my help. He became dismissive of my ideas. He belittled me in front of the children and others.

We used to go out to dinner. We would get a sitter for the kids and go out with his cousins, friends, or family. Soapy wanted to go out and he wanted me to go with him. At the same time, he would say, "You don't know how to relax." But when I'd be having a good time, throwing my head back, laughing, he would reach under the table and pinch my thigh and twist it. He would twist my thigh so hard it would bleed, and then the tears come to my eyes. He'd lean over and say, "What do you think you're doing?"

I didn't understand what I had done wrong. We were out to dinner with another couple. I'm laughing, having a good time. I don't understand. I wasn't dancing on the table. And what if I was, I was with him and that would be fun. Fun was something I did not think I was allowed to do since I became a mother. His whole view of who I should be changed when I became a mother. He'd say, "Why do you want to wear that? You're a mother, a mom."

After a while it started to change who I was. Am I okay? I'm not any fun. I don't know how to relax. And then when I relax that's not good; I am in trouble. I felt like I did back in school when struggling to read and I would get in trouble, now struggling to have this man treat me the way he did when we dated, yet I am in trouble and everything I do is wrong.

He can be very funny, and he is great when he's out. There were times that I would go out despite my anxiety about where to sit, and how to behave, because I thought, oh well at least I'll be out.

There was no winning with him. We were driving across the Verrazano Bridge into the city with our children in the backseat. We were headed to my mother's house for Easter dinner, and Soapy asked, "What do you think she's made of, the Statue of Liberty?" And I immediately replied, "copper."

"Oh, you don't know what the fuck you're talking about." When I went on to explain how copper turns green, he became even more belligerent, so I just stopped talking. As a matter of fact, it was around this time that I just stopped talking altogether.

From then on, whenever he would ask me something, I would answer, "I don't know." "Where do you want to go?" "I don't know." That was the beginning of me losing who I was.

I'm in a family of all Italians. We talk with our hands. We argue, but we love each other. We just want to be heard, so we speak louder and faster. All this loudness is never in anger. We are all just trying to get our point across because it is a big family, and we never get upset with each other.

With Soapy though, I felt like I was always in trouble, that it would be easier to just fade into the background. That's when I started to dim my light, at that moment. I remember that. Of course, it changes you.

I became isolated, which concerned me because I remembered how being isolated had changed my mom.

When Soapy realized I wanted out of the marriage, he started threatening me. "I have judges and doctors in my pocket. My brother's a lawyer and I will take these kids from you and you'll get put away." He continued, "The man with the money has the power, and I am that man." His brother's children live with him. His cousin had the wife institutionalized, claiming that she was crazy, so Soapy's threats seemed very real to me. I feared more than anything to lose my children. It is why I kept trying, hoping there was a way to stay a family.

I was in fear of losing my children not realizing I was losing me. Who was I anymore? My sister would say to me, "Where is that Maria Wall Street?" The tough girl who ran with the wolves was out of steam, sad, and scared.

Eventually, I gathered enough strength to start making plans to leave the marriage. It took three years and over $300,000 to get out of that marriage. It took a lot of strength and I learned a lot of lessons that I'd like to share, that may help other people going through divorce.

Divorce is a process, and I'm sure I could have saved money and saved myself some anxiety and time as well, knowing what I know now. My divorce was finalized in June of 2010.

They say, "Know your adversary," and for about three years, I always had this feeling, although I am extremely positive, I was prepared if there were ever another litigation. I kept myself liquid and sadly in April 2014, I received two devastating pieces of news.

My daughter and I had to move from the marital home when it sold in September of 2011. I had 30 days to find another place to live. We found a nice home to rent in Point Pleasant Beach just a few blocks from the beach.

When hurricane Sandy hit, the National Guard was brought in and we had to evacuate, which we thought would last for two or three days. Our home was flooded though, and we were not allowed back for some time. The damage was so extensive we were not able to move back into our home. I had to make arrangements for our daughter to stay with her dad and brother. I found a hotel that took FEMA vouchers near the children's college in Long Branch, New Jersey.

I had a friend whose condo was for sale, and until it sold, he was renting it. He wanted a lot more than I was paying in rent. I told him the price I could afford to pay was about half of what he was asking.

We lost a lot and I needed a place I could afford. My friend made a deal with me, "Maria, if you show it, you can stay at that price you offered me until it sells, and then you will need to move again."

I needed to get our daughter settled, so I took it. We loved it there. I had friends and everyone looked out for each other. They had a pool and we lived right on the water and would watch the boats going by. Restaurants were all in walking distance, which is perfect for a native New Yorker who is used to walking everywhere.

A year and a half later I get a call from the landlord that this place sold. We had gotten all settled in and happy there. Once again, I had to start looking for another home.

The next shoe dropped when I got a letter summoning me to court. My ex was going to take me to court to reduce my alimony. The alimony was the only money that I received at the time.

I had continued to self-advocate and built great strength to get me through those next challenges.

I'm much better than I was, but there are times that even just talking about that time of my life triggers anxiety and fear.

There are times when I go to a restaurant and I get completely confused about where I should sit. Both of my children have shared this, that it has affected them. We go to a restaurant and we don't know where to sit because we remember that when I was married to Soapy, no matter where we sat, he would have the host move us to another table. Then when we sat in the chair, he would make us get up and change seats. I just never wanted to sit down, because I knew it would be the wrong seat and I may be in trouble.

When I go out with a group of people, it doesn't happen very often and nobody probably notices it because I don't announce it, but sometimes I just stand still. I freeze up with indecision about where to sit.

I am in the process of moving on, and one of the ways to do that is to share my story and help other women.

Lessons Learned. After years of advocating for myself, I learned to seek support from others. I learned that leading a good life requires more than taking action. At times, being still is best as well as taking care of my inner self, and that is a practice for life.

Part Two

I've shared a good deal of my story, and I know a lot of you can identify with a number of experiences I have been through. In this second part of the book, I share the self-advocacy tactics that have helped me overcome obstacles and disappointments to create a life I love. If I can do this, you can too. I believe in you.

Chapter 5. Never Numb the Pain

"It is always by way of pain one arrives at pleasure."

—Marguis de Sade

I had been in the darkness, in the fetal position feeling as if I would die. And, like being in a boxing ring, on the canvas, I knew I had to get up. I had to stand up for myself, my truth, my children, and all of you.

We've got to push through the pain, because it is in pushing through pain that we give birth to our blessing. If we numb ourselves to the pain, through drugs or alcohol or superficial relationships, we not only miss the lesson, we create additional problems—for ourselves and for the people around us.

As a child, I witnessed the way my mother dealt with stress. When my father moved us to New Jersey, my mother lost her support system. She had a very strong family. My grandmother is strong, my aunts are strong. We had the support of my uncles. We had family. We saw our family every day and when we moved, my mother became isolated and no longer had those easy relationships. There was no social media, no FaceTime, and the trek from New Jersey to our old neighborhood took a lot of effort.

My mother did not drive due to her lack of peripheral vision. We'd either have to wait on our father or others to give us a ride, or Mom would have us take the train. She was used to taking the buses and trains since she had worked in Manhattan until my sister was born.

There she was, a new house, a new neighborhood, two daughters to raise, and a husband who was increasingly absent. When my dad left, she was trying to make everything look really nice. She wanted to keep things normal for my sister and me, keep up outward appearances, all while dealing with the abandonment. Then I guess she questioned herself. Looking back, I can see that my mom was having a nervous breakdown.

She had numerous breakdowns, actually. For most of my life, I would say from the time I was the age of eight until my mid-twenties, my mother on occasion would try to take her life. She went on medication, but the medication would numb her feelings and suppress her emotions. She would be manic or depressed and become quiet, withdrawn, sleeping much of the time. The mother I knew in my early childhood was buried so deep inside I could no longer see her or reach her much of the time.

I carried this in my subconscious, or maybe it wasn't buried quite so deeply, because when I became an adult and started facing my own challenges, I was determined not to lose myself to the numbing effects of medication.

I had witnessed others in my neighborhood smoke pot, do other drugs and over-indulge in alcohol. I watched how they acted, and it was not something I liked. Sloppy, sick and even dying as a result. I thought, "Well, I am not going to die. I can better push through if I have a clear head. When I am happy, I celebrate. I will drink, shop, travel, dance and more. I tend to be still and stay focused when I have a challenge, not for any other reason than I do not want to screw up. If I drink or take drugs it may affect my decision making.

The litigation was so uncomfortable and invasive. I always knew that divorce could be hard and now realized this one was going to be very difficult. I decided no matter how bad it was, and there have been times through proceedings that I was in unbearable pain, not physical pain, but emotional pain. I would be crying. I didn't want to deal with the pain.

One day, I was telling the man who was counseling me through that period that even though my ex no longer lived in the house, I would stand at the edge of my bed and cry. I was confused. I didn't know whether to make the bed or not make the bed. Making the bed had always been normal for me. I did it for me, not because people were coming over. I did it for me because it made me feel complete.

Even this simple domestic chore became a trigger for my ex-husband. He would berate me, "All you care about is making the bed! This is bullshit and you don't care about me." I stopped making the bed. I figured, if it's that important to him, I won't make the bed. Like who needs to hear it? It was unsettling though, because it's not really who I was.

When I didn't make the bed for a while, he would blow up at me. "You lazy piece of shit! Look at you." I mean it was from one extreme to another. That is part of the controlling, the constant broadcasting of conflicting expectations.

Even after he was out of the house, I would just stand there at the end of the bed and cry. The trauma had changed my way of being. I had to start pulling the weeds out of my brain. I asked myself, "How do I pull out those negative seeds?" I imagined myself as a gardener. I became the gardener of my well-being and I kept pulling those negative seeds out, and instead planted positive things. I replenished my soul with books and music and a healthy lifestyle and fitness routine. Numbing the situation would have never helped.

The people around me would say, "Maria, well, why don't you just take something, something to take the edge off."

I don't even know the names of some of the drugs out there, but I remember people telling me I should probably get a prescription for one of them. I would reply, "But I know the source of my pain. I know that it's coming from this terrible divorce." I visualized pushing through the pain, like I think of a child pushing through the birth canal, or a dark piece of coal and the pressure that it's under and then it becomes a diamond. I just kept focusing on these pictures in my head, and truly believed that this pain that I was in, that sooner or later it, would go away.

I mean, there were a couple of nights that were difficult for me, but I didn't go out just to distract myself. I didn't want to go out and drink. Why would I want to drink? There was nothing to celebrate. I figured drinking would just make things worse. My belief was that if I weren't in the right state of mind, I could make a mistake and that mistake could affect my children, my family. It could have a downward spiral effect.

Instead of drinking alcohol, I would drink water, take a bubble bath, or read. I would read scripture; I would read anything that was motivating, and just anything that caught my interest. I knew I was weak at the time. Emotionally weak. The most important thing for me was being able to take care of my children. I believed if I made one mistake, my children would be taken from me. I was fearful, because I really didn't know what the outcome of my divorce proceedings would be.

I thought about my husband and realized his goals were no longer my goals, my vision for my life. I just hung onto my vision for my life and I concentrated on taking care of my children. When you numb the pain, it's still there, just suppressed. It's down deep and it stays down deep.

When I say I never numbed the pain, I don't mean I just passively sat on the sofa and accepted everything that came my way, or that I did not react to my circumstances. I was emotional and knew it; it was the most difficult time in my life. I chose instead to feed my soul. Feed my spirit. Feed my body. I became my own advocate and that is what I encourage you to do.

I spent a lot of time in church, where I fed my mind and my spirit.

I know that when you are going through stuff, the best way to heal is to focus out! If you, at any age, feel dead inside or are going through challenging times, go find an organization and give of yourself. You do not need money or talent. Show up and give you, your time, and watch how you start filling up, and your dim light starts to shine once again.

If you are going through a stressful time in your life, make sure to stay engaged with your church or other groups you belong to.

I joined the gym. A lot of people join the gym to lose weight. My objective was to build strength. We all handle stress differently; and when I am stressed, I lose my appetite. I was in so much fear during my divorce. I was afraid of losing custody of my children, and I was afraid of not being able to support myself financially. This affected my appetite and I lost 20 pounds and looked awful.

When I joined the gym, I began to exercise on a regular schedule. Not only did I start to build strength, but my mindset improved very quickly. I would reach a milestone or feel a breakthrough at the gym, and then I would carry that positive experience with me into the other areas of my life. I began to feel more capable and more confident.

At first, people would comment, "Oh, you're so thin," like it was a compliment. But the weight loss wasn't something I chose. I gained about ten pounds back. I still fluctuate a pound or so, here and there. I also focused more on healthier eating. I started to take notice of how I would feel and how my energy was and is. I found, step-by-step, how to live a fun and fabulous balanced life.

I find it funny when people or clients say they cannot afford this or that. Really, can they afford not to eat well, to not take care of the most important gift we are given, our health? Would we rather spend money on health care or at the grocery store? Just like on an airplane, they tell us to put the oxygen mask on ourselves first. We must care for ourselves first so we may care for others.

People started asking me, what is it that you do? They wanted to know my workout routine and I happily shared my process with them. I began to help other people with their transformations. I went from someone who needed help, to someone who could offer help. I learned that we have choices, and I chose to heal and get healthier. The choices that we make can either help us move forward in a positive way or cause us to make mistakes.

I thought that if I numbed the pain, maybe I would end up in an unhealthy relationship. When I started imagining the life I wanted to create, one of my goals was to be in an amazing, loving, connective, euphoric relationship. It was natural, then, that I chose to read things about relationships—healthy relationships and how to achieve them. During my divorce, I felt like I didn't have anything to offer. I had been abused and torn down for so long, my self-worth and my mindset were not very strong. I continued to read the Bible, focusing on the books of Proverbs and Psalms.

I read many versions of the Bible, spiritual and other books. Books by Regena Thomashauer, Kara King, Little Brown, Sherry Argov, James Hollis PH.D, Maya Angelou, Richard Saul Wurman, Deepak Chopra, James Hillman, Simon Sinek, Richard Rudd, Richard Branson, Rhonda Byrne, Eckhart Tolle, and so many more.

I began to see that not only do I have a lot to offer, I deserved to be with someone who would treat me the way I deserved to be treated—with tenderness, compassion and respect. I wanted someone who wanted a partnership and who wanted fun, passion, travel and adventure. Most of all, I wanted someone I feel and know I am safe with. We all get to be safe.

I learned to seek someone who is compatible with me. If I want to meet someone who is physically fit, I too must be fit. What we are seeking is seeking us, and I want a relationship that flows with a likeminded person. How do you do that? I read a lot about men and what they like and what they don't. I wanted to keep that in my thought process. Also working with the Wolves of Wall Street taught me a great deal.

Creating the new life I wanted also included creating the home I wanted. I always had a vision for me since I was little, of creating a home that felt as loving as my grandmother's. I loved not just her house, but the way I felt when I was there. It was always happy and comfortable. Everyone loved her cooking and would comment about the wonderful smells when they walked in the door.

These memories of happy times with family all around are probably why I love to entertain. I always envisioned having a big, beautiful home where I could host dinners and parties. I wanted to make people feel comfortable and be able to offer them whatever they wanted to drink and eat. Of course, that dream includes a partner. Although I was going through a divorce, I still envisioned being able to entertain— with or without a partner. I held onto those images. Although many material things were taken from me, I would not allow my ex-husband, or anyone, to take what I envisioned for my life.

I read cookbooks, design books, and relationship books and looked at the photos in magazines of homes that I wanted. I asked myself how I can be what I am seeking.

During my divorce, I learned to be still. Be still as a monk, and breathe, and not to react (as I have many times which did not serve me very well). My favorite Bible verse is Psalms 46:10. Be Still and Know That I Am God. I have now learned to wait until I can speak articulately. It is not easy to be patient and silent when you are in fear. Those in authority are more likely to believe you when you are calm and articulate, and also are more likely to help you. Otherwise they may think you are a crazy person. When we are in fear, our heart is racing, and we talk fast. This is fear talking, not logic, and it is not taken seriously.

I couldn't change the litigation. I couldn't change my adversary, but I could change me. I'm not saying that there aren't still things that trigger me. Going through the divorce has made me stronger. It's made me smarter. It is the reason I'm writing this book. I am now ready to share the steps that I took, the things that I learned through that process.

Maria's messages for transforming the pain:

- Avoid alcohol when you are sad and emotional, or, at the very least, do not increase your regular consumption. It fogs our judgment and may interfere with decision making.
- Stay engaged with your community or join an outreach group donating your time to others. It is very important to have connection, and getting out of our home gets us out of our head.
- Start a regular exercise routine that works with your schedule and interests. Focusing on our well-being and nurturing ourselves is one of the best things you can do.
- Delay starting any new romantic relationships until at least six months after traumatic events. I am not suggesting you wait as long as I did—I waited till my divorce was final, which took three years. Taking time to heal and love yourself again will bring in a loving relationship. Like attracts like.
- Create a vision for what you want your life to be once you are through the difficult time.
- Surround yourself with images of the life you want to create, whether it is flipping through magazines, creating a Pinterest board or your own vision board. Seeing it, feeling the feelings of it will bring it to you more quickly.
- Read inspiring books or listen to uplifting podcasts.
- Slow down. Wait to respond, whether in person or in writing, until you have calmed down and can organize your thoughts.

Chapter 6. Getting Clear

"People who lack the clarity, courage, or determination to follow their own dreams will often find ways to discourage yours . . . Live your truth and don't EVER stop!"

—Steve Maraboli

For me, being clear, crystal clear, gets me to move forward and stand my ground, no matter what anyone tells me. I have learned that setting boundaries and saying no would help me get closer to what I wanted. In the end, you create your life.

When I was 17, people made fun of the way I looked. I never really took notice until then that my body was out of proportion. I took steps to take control of how it made me feel when the outside world was calling me Bertha Butt or thunder thighs, and singing rude songs to me. Those things certainly made me feel fat and ugly.

My first goal was to lose those thunder thighs. I walked and rode my bike more. I gave up bread and pasta. No one called them carbs back then. Once I started making money on Wall Street, I hired a trainer, and not long after that I found a nutritionist.

The more I learned, the more I did. When I dated my children's dad, he told me he liked to work out. He was thin and he would eat the way I ate until I said "I do." After we were married, he brought home sub sandwiches, chips, lots of pizza, and burgers. There is nothing wrong with that, it is just not what I enjoy, and I would then eat what he ate more than I liked to. Now I am eating what I enjoy again. Working out and eating well is part of who I am.

When I decided to leave my marriage, I knew deep within me what had to be done and what I needed to do. Yes, there were times I questioned myself. The fear would rush in. This was not only about me, and the process started with getting clear.

My husband was physically and verbally abusive. After 15 years, I knew I had to get a divorce. I wanted my life back and I wanted to create a safe home for my children. My husband would yell at me, "**You'll never** divorce me". He would threaten me and again the fear would rush in. It was that fear that I needed to get rid of. To feel and be safe.

Movies like *Diary of a Mad Black Woman* and *Sleeping with the Enemy* taught me you have to have a plan. I was crystal clear. I was going to get divorced and I was going to do whatever it took. Sadly, the divorce did affect the children, I was no longer safe. Safety and freedom are the most important things. I took steps to do what I had to do—get divorced.

I knew that I needed to have money to hire an attorney to divorce my husband, and at the time, I no longer had my own income to pay for one because I gave up my career to raise my family. I had to find money somewhere, something in my name that I could convert into money to hire a lawyer.

No one tells you this, nor was I thinking about it on my wedding day. No one tells you the paperwork that is needed and how you may have to obtain it all. I had to tiptoe around in the middle of the night and became my own advocate in my divorce.

I had to wake up in the middle of the night to go through paperwork. I wasn't looking to steal money. Without money, you don't have the ability to retain an attorney. It doesn't matter if your household income is $100,000, $200,000, a million, if you can't get the money. I was in fear because, had I gotten caught, I was unsure what may happen.

Nearing the end of my divorce settlement, the judge forced us into two separate small rooms in the courthouse with our attorneys and forensic accountant. The attorneys were yelling. The forensic accountant was telling me to take the deal and trying to force me to agree. I was in duress, there by myself in this small room with three large men who were clearly pissed off. They just wanted us to both agree and be done with it. They had no interest in doing what was in our best interests.

I slowly took a breath, and even though I was sweating, and it was hard to swallow, I said, "No, I cannot agree. You are not allowing for the amount I need to pay my taxes (which was about $20,000)."

Again, they tried to force my agreement, and told me "You don't need to worry about that now." If not now, when? I clicked a button on my computer that my dear friend helped me set up. It showed an Excel document in case this happened, and I showed them the numbers did not work. Being clear and having an action plan helped me.

I was legally divorced June 20, 2010. It took me three years and $300,000 to get divorced, and I thought when it was over, I would celebrate. When it was all over, I was exhausted. I just crawled into bed and went to sleep. I was actually sad and full of many emotions. It was best I stayed home.

I got very clear about my career, too. So many people told me, "**you'll never**," and I said to myself, "Okay, well, I'll just do these steps and I'll just get closer and closer to it."

Even at my second company, although the president and the vice president said that they would make me a broker, there was a lot of resistance from the men on the floor. I shut out those voices and just kept trying, and I was recruited by another company that was opening a new department where I went to work. Had I not been crystal clear and taken those steps, I would have never been a broker.

I guess I turned "**You'll Never**" into **I can, I will,** and thankfully, **I did**. That came from a place of sadness and hurt (I'd rather not think about it or admit it). Being told "**You'll Never** divorce me," and I did was not this joyous moment, as I knew my choice changed our family, my children, and it hurt me to see them hurting.

I think about the teachers who got upset with me for having difficulty with reading. They were unwilling to understand or offer help to me. I think about my father's wife and my father for choosing not to help me, not to encourage me and intentionally putting me down.

In 2016, I had heard many people talking about an event in San Diego called ALA. They were saying, "Wow, it's better than a Tony Robbin's event because it is five weekends and four months long. You are transformed."

Someone called to tell me more about Ascension Leadership Academy (ALA) and I agreed to go. Yes, traveling 3,000 miles each way for five weekends, do all the work in between each weekend before heading back to San Diego. Well, at the time I was really not sure what was involved.

I can tell you, however, that I was committed to change. To change my mindset, my ways of being and turning myself back around once again. This was during the time my ex-husband brought me back to court in a false litigation for over four years, depleting most all of my assets.

Going from this fear into freedom and possibilities—I am forever grateful for this program. I recommend everyone go and complete it. Each level gets you closer to possibility. Level 3 on the third weekend is forever embedded in my heart and mind. Everyone should experience it.

I stayed connected to many people I met during the event, via phone calls and through Facebook and I started seeing a change in them.

As I mentioned earlier, every single person in my life advised me to settle in my alimony reduction case. There was something that was unsettling for me because I just wanted to tell my story. I wanted to tell the truth and I knew that I was taken to court falsely.

My ex filed a false motion stating he was broke and needed desperately to reduce his alimony to me. The court should have had him first show documents to prove it before taking $30,000 per year from me and giving it to him then asking for the documents. Why would he care to rush the case to help it move along? He was now making money from me thanks to the court, and he was earning and controlling all the money. The courts gave him more while I lost my assets and so much more. It took close to four and a half years to resolve. The system, the family court in the U.S. is the only court without a jury, which is why they drag these cases on for years. Another club of attorneys helping each other while families are financially taken down. This really needs to come out into the light.

This was a time when I concentrated on really getting clear, and that focus guided me through the entire process.

All the men in the room would say to me, "Just settle. It's no big deal." I looked at my attorney and I said, "Win, lose or draw, if you fight for me, fight for me like I'm your mother, your sister or your cousin, I will be okay with the outcome. Please get me in front of the judge." I had to advocate for myself.

One of my attorneys said, "Maria, if you do not do this now, you're going to keep being in court. You're just going to be in court all the time. Are you ready to fight and stand up for your truth?" It was easy for me to reply, "Yes."

I was committed to not living in my story, doing whatever it took to get out of the story, and to be able to be a stand for myself. This commitment to myself helped me immensely. I got to go in front of the judge. When I was called to the stand and presented with all the things that the adversary tried to bring against me, I would take a breath and I would say to myself, "Own it and tell your truth." There's something inside of you that knows your truth. It is important to not fear and worry about the outcome. Believing that, win, lose or draw, I would have been okay with the outcome was an adjustment and a shift that I had to make in my mindset.

The Judge asked me a question about my education and I just owned it. I said, "I am actually embarrassed to say that I do not even have a high school diploma." And he leaned over and he touched my arm and he looked at me and he said, "Well, what grade did you complete?" In as strong a voice as I could manage, I responded, "I completed ninth grade."

I was embarrassed, and I think he saw that. It was my truth though and I knew I needed to tell it. I continued, "If I could have graduated high school and college and I hadn't given up my career for my family, I wouldn't be here today. I wouldn't be by myself. He wouldn't be taking me to court. I wouldn't have to defend myself. I need this support right now until I get on my feet, until I can make my own money. I gave away everything else for 18 years."

The judge thought through all of it. It took over four years. It was such a relief for me to finish my testimony, because win, lose, or draw, I just wanted to tell the truth. And it felt good once I did, like a huge weight was lifted off my shoulders.

I told my truth and I won my case in its entirety, and my attorney was shocked. He said, "You were tough, and you made me work really hard. I never really thought that you would win your case, Maria. This is a huge loss for your adversary and a big win for you."

Remember, that no matter your outcome, you will be OK. Your circumstances may change. You may change, but you will be OK.

I have also learned that it is important to get clear about what you want in a relationship. First, take a very honest look at yourself, and where your life is at the moment before you even consider entering into a relationship. Are you able to devote the time and the head space and the heart space to another person? Is it the right time to be starting a relationship?

Don't get into a relationship until you heal yourself, because you're just going to draw someone else who is damaged. If you're not healed and you're not clear with what you want, you're better off not putting yourself out there. Just stay with family and friends and surround yourself with people who can lift you up, because your mindset is really so, so important.

I learned to trust myself, to be still, pray, and I learned to ask for help. I am still amazed at all the people God put in front of me. Asking for help and accepting it when offered is invaluable.

Maria's Messages for Getting Clear

- Set aside time to be alone with your thoughts. Take time to clear your head, and time to feel into to what you want moving forward.
- Then ask yourself these questions: What do I really want? What type of life do I want to lead? What do I need to know or do to make it happen?
- Seek out resources and people who can help you reach your goals. Whether that is a lawyer, a coach, or a tutor, you will reach your goals sooner when you surround yourself with people who fill your knowledge gaps and provide encouragement.
- Spend some time alone before entering into a new relationship. If you have gone through a trauma, or have been in a long-term relationship, being alone for a few months or even a year will help you recognize your own likes and desires.
- Once you have become clear about what you want, write it down. Post it where you can see it every day.
- Stay committed to your vision and do not let anyone talk you out of it.

Chapter 7. Make a Plan

"In preparing for battle I always found that plans are useless, but planning is indispensable."

—Dwight D. Eisenhower

Having a plan at any age is key. Whether you want to pass a test, make a team, get a job, or get out of a negative situation. Once you become clear with what you want, it's time to make a plan.

I made my physical transformation when I was 17. I made a decision. I was clear and had a plan. I didn't have much knowledge, but I decided I was going to give up certain foods, and I was going to exercise.

My mom had said, "Oh Maria, you'll never lose that weight on your thighs. It's genetic."

She said, "You know, we're all like that. Look at everybody in the family. Look at, you know, this one and that one." I said, "Well mom, I'll just fight it every step of the way," not realizing that really, you don't have to fight it. You just have to have a plan. My plan was to give up certain foods. I didn't have the knowledge then. I mean, I think the only example back then was Jack LaLanne on TV. There was no YouTube. There was no Google. I just questioned for some reason, because they say things are genetic, are they really? Are our eating habits genetic?

We tend to eat what our parents eat because we don't know any better. I decided I was going to give up bread and pasta, but I did eat rice. I was going to start exercising more. I was going to ride my bike more. I was going to do sit ups and crunches and some leg exercises and walk around more. I was going to do that. It started to work and then I had a transformation.

I was heavier when I dated my children's father. After our son was born, I could not eat much and lost a lot of weight, about 15 lbs. I then had our daughter and slowly lost the baby weight, maybe 10 pounds this time. During the divorce, I lost 20 pounds and my weight fell to 92 pounds at 5'2". I thankfully gained 10 pounds or so back now that I had lost the weight off my shoulders and mind from the litigations.

I lost a little bit of weight and then as I got knowledge and I worked on Wall Street, I got trainers and I learned a lot more. And through the years I've had nutritionists, longevity, doctors, and coaches. I've been blessed to have many, many trainers and I've learned a lot. I have my Pilates instructor, Carol Miller. She's extremely knowledgeable. I have had many trainers around the world and am currently with Bryant Edwards who is helping me strengthen and sculpt to have better overall health. You may find Carol Miller and Bryant Edwards on Facebook or at theatlanticclub.com.

When I got to Wall Street, I had a plan. I knew it would be beneficial, wasn't sure really of the outcome, but I knew that getting a tutor would help. And it helped immensely because I really didn't know why I couldn't read. One day while talking with some of the people in my department, I said, "I'd love to be a broker." My coworkers, all men, started laughing at me. "Maria," they said, "it's a man's world and you're lucky you were invited. **You'll never** be a broker here."

I was shocked and disappointed to hear this. Are they kidding me? I looked around the room and asked some questions. This is when they told me, "You don't get ahead unless you give it!" I pointed to the two women who were brokers and I was told "yes, exactly." I thought, really, that is how they became brokers, they *had to* sleep with someone?

This is crazy, I'll show them, I thought. It lit a fire in me, and I was determined to be a broker. They were correct though. I was not going to be a broker at that firm. I moved my way up into the Bond department and did brokering on occasion until that department head made advances toward me, and I refused him. Ugh. But I kept learning from the different departments they moved me to.

I remember having a teacher who said, "Maria, you need to do your homework in real life, you have homework." My homework on Wall Street was to take my clients to wonderful restaurants, take them to sporting events, take them to Broadway shows and concerts. I was very blessed. I realize that not all people can envision things they have never seen. I look at the Olympians and think, "Wow, if they can beat records that have never been broken, I can do what I set out to do"—and so can you.

My advice for other women is to sit down and make a list of all the things that bring you joy. What makes you happy now or when you were young? Go get a job doing that or create your own business. I taught my children to do what they love and the money will come, and if it didn't at least they would be happy. I know it is not always as easy as that, and easy is not always best. Go for it! I am not saying to quit your job; just start researching and take action steps to get there.

Having a plan helps me reach my goals. Whether that was weight loss, becoming a broker, or going through a litigation, having a plan has kept me focused and successful.

Whatever my goal, I keep envisioning it and I have been blessed. People come into your life and it's amazing what you can learn from them. I met a lovely woman named Maryann at ALA in San Diego, and she said, "Maria, if you want, I'll help you to do certain steps every day." She told me how to envision the outcome I want. "Envision that you're on a call with the judge and envision you're saying, 'Thank you.'"

At this point, I figured why not do as she suggested. So, I envisioned myself on a call with the judge telling me I won my case, and I was thanking him. When I was in court and the judge leaned over and touched my arm, I thought, wow, this is it; this is what I envisioned. Some may think it's silly or crazy, but nonetheless, I WON my case!

I had to have a plan when I was getting divorced. I knew my husband wanted me to just leave without my children and leave with nothing. That wasn't going to happen because of what I envisioned for my life, and how I helped us to be a successful family, I felt that it was not right to leave with nothing.

I had to figure out the steps, and I had to make sure that nobody thought I was crazy. When you go to court or you go to the police station, you better be calm. You've got to write everything down because when you speak calmly, they listen. Otherwise they will think you are a crazy woman and they think you're out to get your husband and you're making up stories. If they don't believe you and they do not write the report correctly, it could go against you later on. You need to stay calm and it's not easy. When you're emotional and you want somebody to believe you and your heart is racing, you're better off calling somebody to talk with you until you get a clear head.

I remember my mom not having the strength to go through litigation and not fighting for alimony because of her inability to speak up for herself, and we struggled because of it. She had to go on food stamps for a short time. Then she got her job back and she worked in Manhattan heading the payments department at The Royal Bank of Canada. But we still didn't live the way we did when we were children. We didn't live well, and I didn't want that for my children or myself. And I thought, "Wow, why should I?" I helped create this. I was part of this. I was absolutely part of my husband's success.

Maria's Messages for Making a Plan

- Research everything you can about your vision. If it is a new home, new career, a car, or a relationship you desire, buy books, watch videos, etc.
- Find people who will help you reach your goals, like trainers or advisors.
- Believe that you can create anything you want. I did and I know you can too.
- Take time during the process to assess how far you have come, acknowledge it, and be proud of yourself.
- Remember to celebrate the milestones. Celebrate you —you are worthy!

Chapter 8. Find the Right Resources

Today we are blessed to have Google and other ways to find information about pretty much anything we need help with. It is easier to search for people you can trust. Again, many people offered to help me just from a casual conversation. I would be at the gym, or out to dinner and someone would overhear me and offer help. It was not something I felt comfortable with. I was in the fight or flight mode during my divorce and trusting others was not easy at first.

Let me share about what I call "Algea's lesson."

At the time Algea was singing at the church. He saw me a few times with my daughter doing outreaches to offer support to a community in Asbury. One day he asked, 'Maria how does it feel to be out here in this community donating your time and supporting all these people?"

"Well, I light up," I responded, and I started telling him in excitement about how wonderful it was and how joyous it made me feel and so on. I love cooking and feeding people. Talking with everyone, hearing their stories, where they were originally from and so on. Handing out food, clothing, and playing games with the children.

"Maria, I want you to listen to me," he paused. "Maria you rob someone of that feeling, that joy when you do not allow them to give to you. You are a blessing and others want to be a blessing to you, so do not rob others of that."

I was surprised and elated. I had no idea. It was me who was not looking at it that way at all. From that moment I learned to accept other people's help, gifts and kindness. It was one of the best lessons I got to hear and learn. I am thankful for that and for Algea.

Resources can be people. I'm from New York and I moved to New Jersey, so I didn't really know many people. I had my sister, but back then, she was going through a difficult time. I have a lot of female cousins. I had a cousin over with my sister one day for lunch, and she knew what I was going through. She looked at me and said, "Maria, you're going to need help. This isn't going to be easy." She gave me very good suggestions and being involved in the community is very important when you need help.

You need to find all types of resources. Although the judge had ordered my ex to attend counseling with me, Soapy no longer wanted to pay after a few sessions. I still needed to talk with someone, though. I guess I needed someone to clarify what I already knew deep down but was afraid to face.

I found a youth center that was free for the first few visits, then I paid a small amount each time thereafter.

When you're isolated and you're getting all these thoughts and worries planted into you, you need to find the right resources to find out what is true. You get to talk about what is happening on the day-to-day and ask questions since I was losing sight of it all. I went to the local youth center in my town and spoke to the counselor, who then led me to find 180 Turning Lives Around. It's an organization that supports survivors and families of domestic abuse.

The 180 advocates meet with women in different locations. 180 helps victims understand the cycle of abuse and provides information about legal rights.

There were also other organizations that I found that were in Monmouth and Ocean County near me that I would go to for resources and help.

I found anybody that I paid for advice didn't protect me, didn't care. They just wanted you to go back every week and talk about the same thing. Everybody's different. I'm not saying there's a right or wrong way, but if I'm going to someone for help, I want to know what it is in me that you see that I can correct. And I want to get to it as quickly as possible. I don't want a 10-year plan. I want an expeditious plan, get better and get on with my life, not relive the past every week. I want to move forward and these counselors had this Freudian way about them. You're confused, upset and asking for help and they'd say, "Well what do you think?" What do I think? I am paying you with all these degrees to tell me. You go to a mechanic and tell him what you think may be wrong with your car; he then doesn't have you figure out the problem. He uses his knowledge and expertise to fix it. It is why ALA San Diego or a Tony Robbins approach is best for me.

Let's get you out of this situation. Or if you believe you can or want to try to save your marriage or relationship, you should absolutely try. The counselor should get to know us both and figure it out. But don't tell me about your degrees and then you're not really getting to the issue. Degrees are great, but I know what the problem is, and expect the counselor to help me or us through it.

There is a counselor I went to in Manhattan. I walked in with my partner at the time and before we sat down, she told us that couple who just left did not stand a chance. "That woman is going to give up everything to travel with my client and move with him." I am thinking, "Did she counsel this woman separately?"

Does she not care about the wellbeing of both who are in her care, or just the man who seemed to be paying? Seeing them separately, she could get to know each of them. After her comment of this couple and the fact that she is a couples counselor and speaker, I was surprised. She then did the same thing with my partner and me. It makes sense to see us together and to also see us separately to get to know each of us. Later on, she was shocked at how things turned out and said, "Oh, that has never happened before." She never got to know me, and I believe if she had, she would have handled and counseled us successfully.

Another time, I literally called this one doctor when I was in a dangerous situation and he just said "Oh, well maybe you should call your pastor, or do you think you can get your husband out of the house?" And that's how I got him out. This doctor never said call the police. Never. He never Zsaid that. And it was really a scary thing. It is why you need to be able to care and advocate for yourself.

I found the best help from my research and referrals from friends then I did from pastors at churches or people that my husband at the time found and paid for. If you're in an unhealthy or abusive relationship, who is paying for outside help? If the counselor has you both in the same room, how are you going to be protected? What are you going to say? If you're the person who's being abused, and you are in front of the person who's abusing you, you can't speak. You can't speak your mind. You're afraid that when you get home, you're going to get hurt again.

It doesn't even make any sense. These are professional people. Don't they know that? And a lot of them are manipulators. Yes. "Do you want to continue on, or do you want to take a break now? Whatever you want to do."

Maria's Messages for Finding the Right Resources

- Take advantage of the free resources for domestic abuse victims. (See the Finding Resource section in the back of this book.)
- Record altercations, if only for your own review.
- Attend counseling sessions with and without your partner. It can be the same counselor if you discuss it up front. If they are not open to that, then maybe they are not the right counselor for you. When you are trying to make a relationship work it gets to work for you both and in your best interest, and wellbeing.
- Talk to other people who have been in your situation. It is helpful and supportive to hear that another has been through what you are going through.
- Ask for the guidance of someone you admire and would like to emulate. It is always my pleasure to guide other women and when you are able you can do the same. It feels very good.

Chapter 9. Never Open the Mail on Friday

"Negativity distracts me from my goal. So I simply don't entertain it. I occasionally laugh at it as well."

—Mama Zara

Never open your mail on a Friday. What do I mean by that? Except the things you cannot change and remove yourself from negative and dangerous situations. Refrain from negative thoughts and fears.

Let's say you have had a really bad day. It's Friday, you're going through a litigation, or maybe something at work is really weighing on you, or you are worried about one of your family members. Don't open your mail. If there is a letter waiting for you that contains bad news, after you get home from work on a Friday night, what are you going to be able to do about it if you can't reach your attorney? They most likely have gone home for the weekend. Waiting till Monday to open the letter and then being able to speak with your lawyer is best. Instead, take time for yourself and enjoy the weekend. I learned this the hard way. During those two days, you have time to get some good sleep, be distracted by a fun activity, and spend time with people who are uplifting. Open your mail on Monday, and you will be ready to tackle any challenges with a refreshed mind.

No one will take care of you better than you. Sadly, there were many times I had to do whatever possible to keep myself safe. I was taught to be kind, to tell the truth, and not to do anything that would disappoint or embarrass the family. I did not actually know what that looked like, and, when in a bad situation, I realized I had to care of myself. I had to go against some of the rules for behavior that were taught to me growing up. In doing so, it helped me survive in junior high school. It prevented me from being raped, and so much more.

If you are having a difficult day, don't make it worse by telling all your friends about it or posting it on social media. Now your friends are saying, "Hey, you know, that's ridiculous. Come on out; let's have a drink. That's what you need." You start drinking when you are feeling down, and you can end up doing something stupid that could make the situation worse. Your friends probably mean well, but sometimes it's better to stay home and wait for the mood to pass than to go out and add to your problems.

It's not always a bad thing to be around people. A good group of friends can remind us of our strengths and be a positive support system.

Once you have the mindset to avoid negative people and situations, make it a point to surround yourself with positive people. My positive influence was my cousin Carmela. She was the one who would say, "Oh my gosh, you're going to write an amazing book someday, and this is just another chapter!" When you're going through a storm, it is really wonderful to have people who allow you to vent.

That's why you might choose to go to a therapist or find outside resources, to be able to vent the negativity. You don't want it to perpetuate. You don't want to be around somebody who is adding to the negativity or be around negative people or negative situations. We all have chapters and moments in our lives that are not so pretty, and I am grateful for the people in my life who have stayed by me in those times, and also now that I am in my new chapter.

There are behaviors to look for in someone that will be a red flag for negative influences in your life:

- You want to avoid people who are controlling, even narcissistic (look up info on these). They want to make all the plans, and have you just follow along.
- Beware of people who put you and others down, even in a joking way, in order to lift themselves up and feel superior to you.
- Watch out for people who never accept responsibility or blame every little thing that goes wrong on someone else, especially you.
- Watch how someone treats the wealthy, the poor, and people who are different from them.

You know, you get to feed yourself with positive things.

I have handled negativity differently during different stages of my life. You learn; you grow. I remember how hurt I was when I was told "**You'll never** amount to anything," by my father's wife. Wow. I'd never heard such a harsh statement directed toward me. I had never really been around that kind of negativity. My family was always very positive. I grew up with my aunts and my grandmother and my mom. I don't remember my dad ever saying things like that. So, when his wife said that to me, I thought, "Oh, I'll show you." That incident may have been part of my drive to work on Wall Street; I was out to prove that woman wrong.

Now I'm to the point where sometimes I don't need to say anything. I just smile if I hear negative comments toward me. I know I just need to follow the steps about being clear and making a plan; then I just smile because I don't really need anyone else to believe in me. I need to believe in myself. It does help when you do have supportive people in your life. It does help to have a cheerleading section. You are strong enough to go it on your own if you have to.

I don't know everybody's journey. I have this saying, "Being right isn't always right." I don't need for others to believe what I believe. I don't need to be right in their eyes. I'm just going to go on my journey and maybe they are right. Maybe it's not going to work out for me. I am learning as I go. If I fall, I will get back up and you can do the same.

When everybody said to me, "Why are you moving? You don't need to move." Sometimes it's not the exact words "**You'll never**" that can be discouraging. No, I don't need to move, but I want to. It's what I envisioned for myself. So, I just smile and say, "Oh yes, maybe you're right." And I smile because it's a limiting belief on their part. Maybe they don't have any ill intention for me by saying that. It's just, they don't see the need in what I want to do, or they feel they're looking out for me.

When you are faced with these types of comments, try to see another's point of view. Their statement could be innocent; it could be out of genuine concern for you. Maybe it is fear-based thinking. When people comment about my desire to move, they know the costs to move and maybe they are concerned for me.

People can comment based on their own limiting beliefs or their concern for you. Or, it could be to keep you small—maybe to keep you from expanding larger than them. During my marriage, I began to feel like I had to dim or put out my light. That was my mistake. Never dim your light. You get to shine.

It's something that I am doing. I'm really putting myself out there, and I am creating the life I want. I envision it. I saw this place where I live now: I walked in and I knew it was it. I went to many other places that weren't it. And, so, I'm packing—I pack every chance I get. I'm making calls and I plan on moving. And if it doesn't work out, it doesn't work out. But at least I know that this is what I envisioned, and I did it and I don't have regrets. I don't want to have regrets. If you feel strongly about something, the way I feel in my gut about this move, then stick with your convictions. If it is a new job, a home, or anything, go for it.

Not only do you have to be aware of the negative influences of the people around you, it is important to refrain from negative talk, especially about others. I don't need to make anyone else wrong for me to be right. We are all expressing our opinions. Appreciate, or at the very least respect, other people's opinions, whether political, religious or otherwise. When we have conversations with people who don't agree with us, we get to hear their point of view, a different and potentially valid point of view.

These exchanges can be an enlightening challenge. When someone expresses a very strong point of view on, say, politics, use this as an opportunity to ask them questions. I like to ask, "Which organization are you with?" "What is it that you go out and do?" "Who do you work with?" "What changes have you made?" "What are you doing to make the slightest change in someone's life no matter who it is?"

The change starts within us and one person can help. I can't help everyone, but I tried to make changes.

Like Willie Nelson once said, "Once you replace negative thoughts with positive ones, you'll start having positive results."

Maria's Messages for Staying Positive

- Avoid situations where you may be tempted to make bad decisions, such as going out alone or on a first date and drinking a lot. Be with friends that have your back, instead.
- Sometimes it's best to stay home if you have had a bad day. Take a bubble bath, order in nice food, watch a movie, read a great book.
- Choose to be around people who support you.
- Keep the words you speak positive and refrain from talking about others.

Chapter 10. Surround Yourself

"Surround yourself with people that want more out of life. That won't settle for average. People that you can connect with on a deeper level. Keep your circle fresh. Keep your circle full of quality rather than quantity. Full of cool ass humans that you can be yourself around. People that fill you up with nothing but love. People that want to see you succeed. People that GET IT. Good circle, good life!"

—Genereux Philip

I can't stress enough the importance of surrounding yourself with people you want to be like. Make an effort to be near the people you look up to. Choose people who would stand by you in bad times.

People do not need to live right by you or see you every day to be a positive influence in your life. My cousin Carmela had moved from our neighborhood in Brooklyn to Italy for a while and then ended up in Florida where I would go visit her and other family often. She and I are very close, and I talked with her almost every day, and she has seen and heard it all in regard to me and my life. I have confided in her for as long as I can remember. She allows me to share, to vent, while she listened and gave good advice. Carmela and her husband, Frank, opened their home to me. Life may get in the way and we may not talk as often. But when we do, we catch up like it was only yesterday. She inspired me to write this book.

I also admired my cousin, Susan. We lived near each other, and she helped a lot when my mother was ill. She attended two years of college and became a secretary at a record company. She wanted to go further and go further.

She was very creative and would make suggestions, and people would listen to her. She lived in Manhattan.

Susan was offered two jobs, one to work for Don Kirshner's Rock Concert television show. The other one was to work with Neil Bogart, the president of Casablanca Records and Filmworks. She chose to work with Bogart and became the first female vice president of any record company.

Susan left New York to take this position in Hollywood. I remember going to see her, and I would visit Casablanca Records and Filmworks. I would see the Village People, everybody on the label. You'd see them dress in their stage clothes, Kiss with the makeup on. Susan went on to become the personal manager to Donna Summer.

My aunt Tina loved to entertain for Susan, and she loved to do the cooking herself. She would be cutting and peeling and chopping and dicing and grabbing people for dinner. There I was, visiting my cousin, and I would find myself in the midst of a real Hollywood party, and Twiggy would walk in.

My cousin made all this happen and I just thought that was exciting. Susan also designed album covers. When I visited her at Casablanca, we'd be walking down the hall and somebody would say, "Oh, when are you going to do that album cover?" There was a spiritual side to her, too.

Originally raised Catholic, Susan was in the very busy music scene and working hard. I remember her telling us about Donna Summer becoming a born-again Christian, and she did not seem to understand it at first. Then months later, she seemed excited about it.

Next time I was in town, Susan took me to their church. Church on the Way. She bought me a Bible and other books, and it was a really amazing experience. It was so simple, so clear how they read straight from the Bible. Near the end of service, the minister asked that we join hands. The whole congregation joined hands and said the Our Father. It was so easy to understand. It was not like people make it.

The whole congregation got together, and I could feel the Holy Spirit. It was really beautiful. That's when I finally got it. I mean, after all those years in a Roman Catholic Church, and they read the homily. At Church on the Way, they just opened the Bible and started reading, and I was like, oh my gosh, that's so simple.

I am spiritual and believe we are all one, so for me it is not what I am saying or what I believe it; is what I do and how you see me act and behave. When people ask, "What are you, what is she?" I am human as are each of you.

When I came home, I started reading the Bible and got more into it. Once I found out that I was dyslexic, I thought, oh, I'll read the Bible. I still have my first Bible.

Watching what Susan was able to do, and becoming a pioneer in that industry—that's what kept me going when I was surrounded by the many packs of wolves. I wasn't deterred when they said, "**You'll never** be a broker because this is a man's world. You're lucky, you were invited here."

Susan was in a male dominated industry, as far as who was in charge. There were female performers, but the decision makers were men. She used to say to me, "It's not only education, it's motivation that gets you where you want to be. Think about all the people with all these degrees. If they are not motivated, they're never going to get there."

I learned from Susan that if you want it, you'll get it. You just have to be motivated to do it. I saw her motivation and she worked hard. She showed up every day.

I remember being with Susan when she bought one of her houses. She wrote a check for that house and I never saw a check for so much money. She bought an English castle in the Bel Air Gates and it was a beautiful house. She was just a regular kind of person.

I saw Susan last year when my aunt turned 90. We all got together, and it was wonderful to see all of our family. Susan set precedents, and I admire that.

My cousin Susan is still in the music business in Nashville. She works with Tony Orlando and a lot of the older groups, and she manages a comedian and one actress. I saw her in New York not that long ago with Debbie Boone, who was performing at The Carlyle.

First thing Vinny said to me on the interview at Fundamental Brokers was, "You have to be here on time every day and you have to put up with the locker room talk. Think you can do that?"

I said, "I can do that," because here I was, I had no education. That's all I needed to know. I couldn't believe it. It was like they were spelling out my career for me and all I had to do was show up. And I'm thinking, you're going to teach me all of this. That's all I had to do, be in the place I wanted to be and soak up what the people around me had to say.

Maria's Messages for Surrounding Yourself with Positive People

- Look around you at the people you already know. I know I have said this before, and it is worth saying again. You are worth having quality people in your life.
- Is there someone working in the field you want to pursue? Do you see someone creating the life you would like to lead? Ask them about the steps they took. Most people our honored to support you.
- Attend industry events. Go to conventions and other places to meet others who are willing to share their knowledge.

Chapter 11. Anything is Possible

Planting Seeds (Good Seeds and Bad Seeds)

"You were designed for accomplishment, engineered for success, and endowed with the seeds of greatness."

—Zig Ziglar

I am the perfect example of "Anything is possible." I was told over and over, "Maria, **you'll never** . . ." and I turned other people's impossible seeds into all that I made possible, and if I can do it so can **you!**

When you want to harvest good crops, you plant good seeds, in rich soil. You water and care for them and in return they will produce abundance. The opposite is true if you plant bad seeds in bad soil.

Our words are seeds. "Life and death are in the power of the tongue." (Proverbs 18:21) Let's speak life into our children and to all, as far as it depends on us. I say this as I know first-hand how it feels and how I could have turned out if I allowed what was said to me to take root. "Maria will never amount to anything. She can't read. She is an idiot. Maria you'll never get a job in New York." **YOU'LL NEVER, YOU'LL NEVER, YOU'LL NEVER . . .**

It's not only education, but motivation that gets you where you want to be. I have met and know many people who have graduated from Ivy League schools and could not find good jobs. They were more than qualified. Maybe the job was not what they were passionate about, or their parents told them what they should do and be when it has to come from you, what makes you happy. Then you will be motivated.

When I was younger, I was told "**You'll never** get a job in the city. You don't have a high school diploma. How are you going to get a job? **You'll never** get that trainee position." I turned it into possibility because I had no fear at that age. I had no fear prior to that. I got crystal clear about what I wanted to do, because I thought with that subway token, instead of getting on the bus to go to the other side of Brooklyn to make a little bit of money, I had a vision of making more money in Manhattan.

I was going to make that possible. It was me. I was going to make it possible and nobody believed, but I could do it. So, I made that possible. If I didn't, I guess they would have been right, and I would have stayed in Brooklyn.

There were times during my divorce that I really didn't know what was possible. I was scared. I was literally in fear. I was really in fight or flight mode most of the time. But I knew I had to push through that. I had to push through that fear and pain. It was there. It was real. It was like being in the ring with Mike Tyson, because no matter how many times I got knocked down, I had to get back up.

I was scared. It was like I looked at my ex-husband and he was Mike Tyson at the time. I feared him. I had to think clearly, and it was not easy. I had to make it possible to get out of that situation because there was no other choice. I stay in that ring and I deal with that feeling every day or I push through it and get over it and get past it. Thankfully, I did and I am here to tell my story because there wasn't another option. I could not live like that another day. It wasn't living. I was stifled. I wasn't myself. I couldn't smile. I couldn't laugh. I couldn't be me. And it didn't feel natural, wasn't authentic. Most of all, my children were not seeing me. Heck, I did not recognize myself and did not like that I allowed myself to change. I still feel bad about it and practice forgiveness.

Being free allowed me to be my authentic self and doing whatever it takes to get that, to have that. We live in a country where we are so blessed to have our freedom. I found myself in a situation where I had to have a plan. It took a long time and I doubted myself numerous times. I went to lawyers throughout the marriage trying to make the right decision. Should I wait? Should I not?

If you're independent and you're financially able to care for yourself, know that you're worth so much more. If you can financially take care of yourself, then close that door and get rid of that toxic relationship. I used to say, "I'm allergic to him." Until I got rid of that toxicity, how would I be able to let in joy and let in love? If you're financially able to take care of yourself, get the hell out. I stayed for a long time wanting to keep my family together. If you do not have children and are married, you get to be free.

It really changed who I was when I got the job on Wall Street because it really gave me confidence. I didn't have that before. My friend David really saw the change in me. David and I met when I was 17. He told me, "Maria, I hardly noticed you. You walked with your head down and really didn't say much. You just tagged along. Then all of a sudden you got this job and you have this personality. I was so drawn to you." We're still friends today.

I made that possible and I gained confidence. You gain confidence when you work out your body, too. Working out transforms your mind as well. Your body physically changes, and your mind changes along with it.

Our military is an example, our police and firefighters. The first thing they do is they go to boot camp. Although it changes their physical self, it is for when they are on the battlefield, on the streets, or fighting a fire, they have a strong mind. Our military starts with boot camp which may seem just physical, but it's also helping them learn how to take care of the person to the right of them and the person to the left of them. Because if they don't do it, they're out. When you work out your physical body, you do a workout on your mind as well, and it makes things possible.

Maria's Messages for Making Anything Possible

- If I can do it, so can you. You are worthy of having the life you want.
- Listen to your own voice, and advocate for the life you want.
- Parents be very careful of the words you speak and the messages you send to your child and to others. Plant seeds of possibility.
- Remove yourself from situations where you have no opportunity to grow, whether that is a relationship or a job.

Chapter 12. Expand and Grow

"Without continual growth and progress, such words as improvement, achievement, and success have no meaning."

—Benjamin Franklin

We are here to be expansive, ever growing and evolving. Since I found out that I was dyslexic, I became like a kid in a candy store. I wanted to learn more and more. It was not always easy, and to this day I am still learning how to learn. I am constantly learning new techniques so I may retain more. I now practice juggling since I took a course with Jim Kwik. I am still working on adding the third ball. You have to want to do whatever it takes.

Also, focus out. There truly is never a bad time to focus out. I had a choice to stay in and focus many times on the things I was going through, or get out of the house and focus out with love and passion to make someone else's day better. When I started focusing out, it was more for me.

I was forbidden to work once my children were older. My ex-husband would say, "You don't need to work. Why do you want to work, so someone will pay attention to you?"

I wanted to feel a part of something and make a contribution. I also wanted to have my own money since my husband had control over the checkbooks. He was always saying, "We don't have it now," or "We can't afford it." Yet, we'd go to dinner with his cousin and he'd spend crazy money.

I wanted to continue to expand and grow because I felt stifled. I felt like I was in trouble. I was bored. If I needed to expand my mind, then I would be reading things. He goes, "Well, you know, this is why they say women shouldn't read."

He wanted to keep me down. I had our children, so let me prioritize what's important. Let's not get him upset. It was never going to work. It's like cutting off the wings of a butterfly. Okay. It just wasn't going to work for me. I felt like my oxygen supply was being cut off. Everybody needs to continue to expand and grow.

I thought it would be okay to work at a church. I found a local church that had a soup kitchen. My ego thought I would be a blessing to these people. I made fresh soup and sandwiches at my home and took them to the church. At the time, there were eight elderly people there. I'd go around the table and ask if they had prayer requests. We'd eat and share stories. It became very clear that it was not I who was the blessing, it was these amazing, wise people who were a blessing. The experience touched a part of me I never felt before. It became like a drug. I was so filled up each week that I wanted to do more. The soup kitchen grew and grew. My motto and mantra are, "I Am Blessed to Be a Blessing."

With knowledge I became a broker. That was expanding myself. I've been expanding myself since I was little. The situations and the things I saw that were positive and negative in my life have definitely helped me expand and grow. When I would see certain people, like my aunts, my grandmother, I saw strength in them that I wanted to emulate. I would ask myself how I could do that. Then I saw weaknesses. Like I saw the weakness in my mother, which gave me strength, gave me strength to stand up and say, "Okay, I'll watch her. I'll take care of her. I'll do the cooking." I'd ask my sister Angela, "Why don't you do the cleaning?" We worked together to help our mother. Taking care of my mom and the household gave me strength.

I have always liked being needed. When my ex wanted help in his career, I was excited to do it. I wanted to be a part of a team. I wanted to help us expand and grow together. Once he became successful, he pushed me aside. He no longer needed me, and he didn't value me anymore because he chose not to see me in the same light. So, I no longer wanted to be a part of that. We had been expanding and growing together. Interestingly, though, he did not want me to read. He did not want me to go back to work.

Expanding and growing doesn't always mean to make more money. It's just finding what brings you joy, whatever that may be. It could be taking an art class. Maybe you want to take singing lessons. I have a girlfriend, a retired nurse, who is taking dance lessons. Her husband loves it because she comes home, she's in a good mood. She has something to talk about.

Jersey Shore Dream Center.
Here supporting the community with clothing

Outreach in Asbury Park, New Jersey

United Nations NYC raising funds for Africa

I want to learn until the day I take my last breath, because knowledge when shared is power. Knowledge isn't power if you keep it to yourself. Share it with the world and help others to grow and expand. That is focusing out. Be the ripple, a ripple effect kind of thing.

I was able to do that, expand and grow, when I was a founding member of the Jersey Shore Dream Center. We began by giving away bottles of water and expanding our outreach to gathering and distributing 30,000 pounds of food a year. We started with canned goods and then added hot meals. We prepped meals all week. My daughter came with me until she went off to study abroad.

When the kitchen wasn't being utilized, I asked if I could teach home economics while my daughter was away in Italy for four months. I asked if I could teach the children home economics because cooking is one of my skills, so why not share that? Sharing helps me to grow more. It gives me great joy.

I wasn't making any money, I just loved it and I loved watching the children's faces and getting them together to just teach them things, like where to put the napkin. We said a prayer and it was just simple stuff. It was a wonderful and rewarding experience for focusing out.

Maria's Messages for Expanding and Growing

- Acquiring skills is the best way to expand your life, as does sharing the skills you already have.
- Continue to learn until your last breath.
- Think of one resource you would not want to live without and find an organization that gives support in that, and join them by donating or giving of your time.
- It doesn't always have to be about money. You may give your time to help another human being grow, and in turn you too will grow and cause a ripple effect.

I would like to share how grateful I am for each person and circumstance that came into my life. I am thankful and know it all happened for me so that I may share my journey to self-advocacy with you.

It is in the writing of this book that I realize the only time I walked away or let go of something that was important to me was when I no longer felt safe, when it was not in my best interest to stay. We get to know that when we are not safe, we can advocate, and push through it to be free.

I am Maria, and I am a self-advocacy coach™ for women, supporting them to have the life they want. Advocating for your health is the first step, and the rest follows. Without your health there may not be other steps.

Advocate for your career, equal rights and equal pay. Advocate for the love you want, which starts with self-love. It is my life's purpose to advocate for women's safety. Every woman gets to feel and be safe—in school, in the workplace, in their homes, and in all relationships. I support you one on one, and in a small group. For more information, go to my website at mariamastrodicasa.com and someone on my team or myself will connect with you.

I offer quarterly empowerment retreats for women in cooperation with my business partner Gabriele Howard. We co-create experiences for women in a relaxing environment that creates momentum and inspiration. We offer fabulous fun with like-minded women. The retreats are also filled with workshops about advocacy, vision, health coaching, and mindset. We are dedicated to empowering women and offer tools to help them create the life they want and are worthy of. For further information simply follow us on our website at www.gmretreats.com.

Finding Help

Dyslexia

Learn what dyslexia is:
www.dyslexiaida.org/definition-of-dyslexia
The Dyslexia Resource Reading expertise from The Schenck School:
www.dyslexiaresource.org/
Understand how dyslexic students learn differently:
www.dyslexiahelp.umich.edu/professionals/dyslexia-school/tips-tools-and-apps-for-helping-dyslexic-students

Assistive technology for dyslexic readers

ClaroSpeak text to speech:
www.clarosoftware.com/portfolio/clarospeak

OCR InstantlyPro
Image to text:
www.play.google.com/store/apps/details?id=com.thesimplest.ocrpro

Mind mapping software to aid organization and decision-making:

www.mindlyapp.com/?utm_source=zapier.com&utm_medium=referral&utm_campaign=zapier

https://zapier.com/blog/best-mind-mapping-software/#scapple

Resources

180 Turning Lives Around
www.180nj.org

National Domestic Violence hotline:
www.thehotline.org
1-800-799-7233 or TTY 1-800-787-3224

National Suicide Prevention Lifeline
1-800-273-8255

Proven Drug and Alcohol Rehab
1-844-255-4490

Addiction Hotline
1-844-842-5830

Break the Cycle - Recognize the Signs of Domestic Abuse:
www.breakthecycle.org/warning-signs

Jersey Shore Dream Center
www.jerseyshoredreamcenter.org

Ascension Leadership Academy (ALA)
www.alasandiego.com

Dallas Michael Cyr, Ignite Your Purpose
www.ignitingyourpurpose.com

Lifespan Medicine
www.lifespanmedicine.com

Common Ground Bereavement Center
www.commongroundgnefcenter.com

Further Reading:

Read about the *BIG 5 U.S. SECURITIES DEALERS* **in the June 9, 1983 edition of the New York Times.** https://www.nytimes.com/1983/06/09/business/big-5-us-securities-dealers.html

Reading list

Letter to My Daughter—Maya Angelou

The Queen's Code—Alison Armstrong

Having It All—John Assaraf

Screw It, Let's Do It—Richard Branson

The Gifts of Imperfection—Brené Brown

The Magic—Rhonda Byrne

The Secret—Rhonda Byrne

Hero—Rhonda Byrne

The Gift of Fear—Gavin de Becker

The Power of Intention—Dr. Wayne Dyer

I Get To—Alicia Dunams

Everything is Figureoutable—Marie Forleo

Think and Grow Rich—Napoleon Hill

The Soul's Code—James Hillman

What Matters Most—James Hollis

Girl, Stop Apologizing—Rachel Hollis

Girl, Wash Your Face—Rachel Hollis

The Power of the Pussy—Kara King

Gene Keys—Richard Rudd

Leaders Eat Last—Simon Sinek

Together is Better—Simon Sinek

Pussy—Regena Thomashauer

The Power of Now—Eckhart Tolle

UnderstandingUnderstanding—Richard Saul Wurman

Book Club Discussion Questions

1. Do you have any memories or references to what life was like in the '80s?
2. How do you think working conditions for women have changed since the time Maria spent on Wall Street?
3. What advice would you have given to Maria as she began her career?
4. How would you have advised Maria during her marriage?
5. What would you do if a coworker confided in you that she was being abused?
6. How would you handle it if a male coworker was inappropriate?
7. Have you ever advocated for yourself or a loved one? If so, please share.

About the Author

A former Wall Street broker, Maria Mastrodicasa is an international speaker, author and Self-Advocacy Coach™. Maria's life-long commitment is that all women feel safe and valued in school, the workplace, and the home. With 20 years of philanthropic experience, Maria is the founding member of *The Jersey Shore Dream Center*, a donor for *Common Grounds* nonprofit, and a board member for *The Guild of Ocean Medical Center.*

Interested in booking Maria Mastrodicasa for speaking engagements, book clubs or events? Email her at maria@mariamastrodicasa.com and visit www.mariamastrodicasa.com.

Made in the USA
Middletown, DE
18 June 2020